SURVIVING THE STRUGGLE

Divided Families in America

By
Fulton J. Titus

Atlas Press Publishing, LLC

Unleash Your Success: Mastering the Habits of High Achievers

Believe in your unique abilities and qualities, for they make you a truly exceptional individual. Take charge of your life and unlock your true potential with the powerful strategies and tools outlined in this book. Embrace the journey of self-discovery and transformation and learn how to overcome obstacles like a top performer. This is your chance to take your life to the next level and achieve your wildest dreams. Don't wait any longer, seize the opportunity to unleash your success today!

By: Fulton J. Titus

A Message of Love and Gratitude to My Children

To my dear children Sephora, Logan, and Savannah,

This book is a testament to the power of hard work and dedication to one's craft. My personal journey has demonstrated that success is achieved through tenacity and dedication towards our goals. When we commit ourselves to our passions with unshakable persistence, the fruits of our labor will naturally follow, including financial rewards. I am grateful to my three loved ones, whose great support has been the foundation of my success. Your love and inspiration have shown me a new perspective on the world, and I am honored to share this book with you as a symbol of our family bond. My hope is that this book inspires you to pursue your dreams with the same passion and resolve that I have, knowing that the rewards will come with perseverance. The future is full of possibilities and I am grateful to be your parent, excited to witness the incredible journeys that lie ahead for each of you.

SURVIVING THE STRUGGLE

Divided Families in America

Atlas Press
- PUBLISHING. LLC -

By

Fulton J. Titus

Acknowledgments

I am incredibly thankful and grateful for the unwavering support and dedication of Atlas Press Publishing in bringing this book to fruition. Their expertise, guidance, and resolute commitment to excellence have been pivotal in making this project a reality. Working with their professional and detail-oriented team has been an honor, and I am proud to have had the opportunity to collaborate with such a fantastic group of individuals.

I am particularly appreciative of the freedom and trust given to me by Atlas Press Publishing in writing about topics that are important to me to shed light on crucial issues in social science. Their constant support and trust have allowed me to delve into topics that are often overlooked but have a significant impact on our communities. In regards to this publication, I am confident that this book will be a valuable contribution to the literary landscape and will help highlight on important issues that matter to so many.

Contents

PREFACE

This book, titled "Surviving the Struggle: Divided Families in America" delves into the complex and often misunderstood world of black families in America. This manuscript aims to provide a comprehensive understanding of the unique struggles that black families face and offers insights into how we can build a more equitable society that supports the well-being of all families.

The inspiration for this story comes from the author's personal experiences as a full-time dad of two children and fighting to stay in the life of his oldest daughter, who is being raised by her mother. Through his journey, he realized the need for a deeper understanding of the systemic factors that contribute to the struggles of black families.

This book is not just based on research and theories; it is grounded in the reality of the author's personal experiences and those of other black families. The challenges faced by black families in America are wide-ranging, including poverty, discrimination, and systemic injustice. These challenges can lead to a breakdown in family structures, a lack of support and resources, and poor outcomes for children's emotional and psychological well-being.

Throughout the publication, the author addresses critical issues such as the role of fathers, the impact of trauma on families, and the importance of healthy co-parenting relationships. The impact of worrisome attitudes towards fathers and the need for greater support and resources for black mothers are also explored.

The hope is that this literary work will spark conversations about the challenges faced by black families in America and the need for a cultural shift in attitudes towards family structures. It is time for us to recognize the importance of family and to work together to create a more just and equitable society that supports the well-being of all families.

Join the author on this journey as we explore the challenges, triumphs, and complexities faced by families in America. While this book focuses on the experiences of black families, the insights and lessons discussed can apply to families of different races, cultures, political affiliations, and religions. By recognizing the common struggles and systemic factors that affect families, we can work towards creating a more just and equitable society that supports the well-being of all families. Let us come together to maneuver the challenges and promote the importance of family in our society.

INTRODUCTION

F atherhood is an important aspect of family life that contributes significantly to the emotional and psychological well-being of children. Fathers play a critical role in shaping their children's beliefs and values, and in providing a positive role model for their children to follow. However, for black fathers, the journey towards executing their role as a father can be fraught with challenges and obstacles.

One of the most significant obstacles faced by black fathers is the negative perception of them in society. This perception is often perpetuated by stereotypes and cultural tendencies that portray black fathers as absent or neglectful. However, research shows that this sorrowful image is not only sustained by external forces but can also be influenced by a mother's treatment of the father.

Mothers hold a lot of power in shaping their children's beliefs and values, particularly in single-parent households where the father is absent or not fully present. In such situations, the mother is the primary caregiver and has a significant influence on the child's perception of the father. This influence can either be beneficial or detrimental.

Unfortunately, some mothers may unknowingly sabotage the image of the father in their children's eyes. Distressing attitudes towards the father figure can lead to hurtful outcomes for the child's emotional well-being and development.

Research shows that when a mother holds damaging attitudes towards the father, it can lead to the child developing pessimistic attitudes towards his father as well.

The impact of unfavorable attitudes towards the father can be detrimental to the child's emotional well-being, as they may feel a sense of loss and abandonment. Children need positive relationships with both parents to develop healthy emotional bonds and build resilience. Thus, it is essential for mothers to be mindful of their words and actions towards the father, as they can have a significant impact on the child's perception of the father.

On the other hand, mothers who promote positive attitudes towards the father can help to strengthen the child's emotional bonds and contribute to their overall well-being. By encouraging positive co-parenting relationships and fostering open communication, mothers can help mitigate the damaging effects of an absent or neglectful father and provide their children with a strong foundation for healthy relationships in the future.

It is important to recognize that fathers have an essential role to play in their children's lives, and mothers should encourage their involvement and support their efforts to be positive role models and advocates for their children. When both parents work together, they can create a more supportive and stable environment for their children to thrive in.

For black fathers, the journey towards meeting their role as a father can be challenging, but it is a journey worth taking. Black fathers have historically faced unique challenges and obstacles in raising their children, including undesirable labels, cultural partiality, and systemic injustices. However, it is crucial to recognize the importance of their role as caregivers and influencers and to support them in their journey.

From the legacy of slavery to modern-day policies and laws, the US government has played a significant role in perpetuating poverty, discrimination, and injustice within the black community. This publication probes into the historical and contemporary examples of how the US government has contributed to the breakdown of black families, resulting in increased rates of single-parent households, poverty, and incarceration. The author provides a critical analysis of the root causes of these challenges, including racism, classism, and institutional bias.

Moreover, the book explores the role of anger and revenge in the lives of black individuals and families. Due to the pervasive injustices they face, black individuals may experience feelings of anger and resentment towards the system, their neighborhood, and even their own families. The author examines the psychological effects of these emotions, highlighting the impact they can have on the well-being of black families.

Furthermore, the writing addresses the role of the society in breaking the cycle of anger and revenge. It calls for a shift in attitudes towards forgiveness, healing, and reconciliation within the black fellowship, emphasizing the importance of building strong support networks and healthy co-parenting relationships.

The author of this book does not only provide insights from research and ideas but shares his personal story as a single father of two kids and fighting hard to stay present in the life of his oldest daughter who is being raised by her mother. He understands the challenges faced by black fathers and the struggle to stay in the life of their children, especially when the child is being raised by the mother. His personal story will shock you and bring to light the harsh reality of the obstacles that many fathers face.

This publication is a call to action for society to prioritize the needs of children and to recognize the important role that both parents play in their upbringing. It is a reminder that the well-being of children should always come first, and that healthy co-parenting relationships and communication are essential for their emotional and psychological health.

Through this manuscript, readers will be inspired to join the conversation and take action to support all families. It is not just a book for black fathers or mothers, but a writing for everyone who cares about the future of their children and society. Let us work together to create a brighter future for all children, regardless of their family structure or background.

CHAPTER ONE

Help Wanted: Fathers

F atherhood is an important and sacred role, but it's often undervalued and ignored in society today. This is especially true for black fathers, who face a number of unique obstacles that make it difficult for them to fulfill their responsibility. These challenges include harmful labeling, government programs that compromise fathers, unfair judgments, and a lack of recognition as caregivers. As a black father, the weight of societal expectations can feel like a heavy burden to bear. We are often expected to be strong, stoic figures, providing for our families and protecting them from harm. Yet, the reality is that we face our own set of exceptional trials and struggles, both as fathers and as black men in America. It can be hard to juggle our responsibilities as caregivers and providers while still meeting society's expectations of what we should look like.

As a devoted father of three, with sole custody of my two youngest children for close to 5 years now, one of whom has special needs, the topic of Black fatherhood holds a significant place in my heart. Through my personal experiences, I have come to realize the unusual hardships that Black fathers face, including the pervasive harmful preconceptions and prejudices embedded in society that make it difficult to be viewed as a positive role model or even a capable caregiver. It is frustrating to receive phone calls from doctors' offices and schools that assume I am not the primary caregiver for my children, simply because I am a Black father. This is just one example of the kind of discrimination and bias that Black fathers experience in our society.

Despite these challenges, I am committed to being an involved and responsible father, and I know that there are many other Black fathers who feel the same way. It is time to challenge the generalization and structural biases that hold us back and to promote a more positive and inclusive image of Black fatherhood. That being said, we can help to create a more supportive and nurturing environment for all Black fathers and their families, and ensure that they have the resources and support they need to thrive.

Moreover, despite my unwavering commitment to being an involved and present father to the point of going to court many times to enforce my visitation rights, I have still encountered many of the same feelings and hardships that are commonly associated with absent fathers. As a Black father, I am often expected to overcome additional obstacles and prove my worthiness in ways that other fathers of different races may not. This is especially true in the case of my first daughter, who, following our divorce, continues to be raised primarily by her mother.

As a Black father, my personal experiences have shed light on the complexities and challenges that come with the role of fatherhood in our society. In spite of being a model father and fighting for my rights in court, I encountered pessimism and bias from lawyers and judges who assumed the worst about my intentions. I fought tooth and nail to stay involved in my daughter's life, eventually succeeding in getting supervised visits and then full visiting rights. I know what you are thinking! I want to make it clear that I have never been convicted of a felony or engaged in any form of abuse towards my ex-wife or daughter. I am simply a caring father. But a decade later, I still feel a sense of distance from my daughter, leading me to question what happened. Was it her upbringing? Did the societal prejudice and inclinations against Black fathers have an impact? These are the questions that haunt me as I continue to pilot the intricacies of Black fatherhood, but I remain committed to being the best father I can be for all of my children. As I write about my personal experiences as a father, it is my hope that by sharing my story and perspectives on this issue, I can inspire other fathers to embrace their roles with pride and perseverance.

In America, there is a commonly used saying "hurt people hurting people", which has been on my mind as I try to understand the root of the issues with my oldest daughter and to some extent, my other children. I can't help but wonder if my oldest daughter had to endure countless misconceptions and injurious talking points about me courtesy of her mother. Sooner or later these adverse depictions will be corroborated at the slightest sign of disagreement between father and child which inevitably will happen especially in the teenage years.

As I ponder the complexities of family dynamics including mine, I can't help but draw comparisons to the ebbs and flows of a river. Sometimes the water flows smoothly, but other times it crashes against the rocks with a fierce intensity. The hurt of a mother can be like the force of the water, eroding away at the foundation of the black father's image. On the flip side, the hurt of a father can also have a devastating impact on the family, like a storm causing destruction in its wake. But it seems that society only sees one side of the story, like a distorted reflection in a funhouse mirror. When a father speaks out against the mother, his words are dismissed as mere grumblings. Yet, when a mother speaks out against the father, her words carry weight, as if imbued with some kind of magical "goodwill" that fathers don't possess. This is not to say that black fathers should be let off the hook for their responsibilities, but rather to shed light on the fact that the image of the black father is often shaped and influenced by single mothers in the household, creating potential complications and misunderstandings.

As we cope with the complexities of single parenthood, it is crucial to acknowledge the struggles and challenges that mothers encounter when raising their children alone. My heart goes out to these strong and resilient individuals, particularly black mothers who face additional societal obstacles. Nonetheless, it is important to recognize the fathers who are waiting in the wings, yearning to step up and provide for their children, but are being thwarted by the mother's resentment and anger from a failed relationship. It's as if the mother's emotions have taken on a life of their own, becoming an insurmountable barrier for fathers who are simply trying to be present in their children's lives.

It is ironic that mothers, who are typically seen as nurturing and caring, can be the cause of so much trouble when it comes to co-parenting with fathers. The term "baby mama drama" has come to be used to describe the often toxic behavior of some mothers, making it nearly impossible for fathers to have a meaningful relationship with their children. This can lead many fathers to give up or even relocate out of state in an effort to avoid the situation. This kind of behavior reinforces the biased generalizations that black fathers are uninterested in being involved in their children's lives, even though many are actively seeking to do so. It is unfortunate that media representation further reinforces this assumption by often portraying black fathers as absent or uninvolved. It is vital to recognize the efforts of fathers who desire to be present in their children's lives, despite facing numerous challenges and obstacles along the way.

I have heard numerous accounts of mothers making it incredibly challenging for fathers to see their children due to the actions of their ex-partners. For example, a friend of mine has been fighting for months to establish regular visitation rights with his daughter, but his daughter's mother has repeatedly blocked his attempts and created barriers to prevent him from spending time with his child. Despite his persistence and dedication, he has been met with hostility and resentment, ultimately causing him immense emotional pain and distress. It is heartbreaking to see how this kind of behavior can tear apart families and paint black fathers as being disinterested in their children's lives.

The topic at hand presents a perplexing conundrum, as society has long castigated these fathers as despicable, yet these same fathers can often excel as stepfathers. Given that black mothers predominantly date black men, many of these so-called bad black fathers have been asked to step up and become stepfathers, and they have overwhelmingly risen to the challenge, providing excellent care and support for their stepchildren. For instance, the renowned actor and comedian Steve Harvey has been a standout stepfather, demonstrating remarkable commitment and devotion to his wife's children from a previous marriage. Similarly, former NFL player and accomplished actor Terry Crews has been a superb stepfather to his wife's child, going above and beyond to ensure their well-being and happiness. And basketball legend Shaquille O'Neal is on record as having been a fantastic stepfather, providing unwavering love and support to his wife's children.

Therefore, it is incumbent upon us to continue discussing this important topic, seeking ways to bridge the gap between biological fathers and their children and establish proper relationships that benefit all parties involved. To achieve this goal, we must first break down the preconceived notions and impediments that make it difficult for black fathers to be present and engaged in their children's lives. This can be accomplished by acknowledging the peculiar conditions that black fathers face, advocating for fair custody arrangements, and providing support and resources to fathers who are committed to being involved in their children's lives.

As a complex issue that touches upon a range of societal and cultural factors, the struggles that black fathers face cannot be fully addressed or resolved by any single individual. However, I am committed to offering a different perspective on this topic, with the hope of stimulating a much-needed conversation and deepening our collective understanding of the unusual hardships, challenges and complexities that black fathers encounter. Despite the deleterious narrative that the media and society have maintained around black fatherhood, I have personally witnessed the tremendous dedication and commitment that black fathers have for their children. This chapter will look into some of the emotional and psychological impacts that the mother's treatment can have on black fathers and their children, examining how this dynamic can influence and shape their relationships.

Black fathers are often confronted with a dizzying array of societal and cultural obstacles that make it challenging for them to be fully present and present for their children. The truth is that many black fathers are not treated fairly, and I can speak from personal experience. The double standard that mothers are not held accountable to the same degree as fathers is an evident injustice in the way society perceives and treats black fathers. While mothers' pain is acknowledged and understood, fathers' feelings are often disregarded, leaving them to face rejection and misunderstanding from their children.

As a responsible single father of three, I have experienced rejection from my older daughter for reasons I didn't comprehend at the time, and it was deeply hurtful. Unfortunately, the harmful preconception of the absent black father persists, creating a self-fulfilling prophecy to some that black fathers are simply "sperm donors" and incapable of being a regular father. This cliche is further propagated by media representation, which often portrays black fathers as uninvolved or completely absent.

One of the challenges that black fathers face is the lack of recognition as viable caregivers. Society tends to assume that only mothers can be the primary caregivers, leaving fathers to be seen as "secondary" parents. This is also true in family court, where mothers are often granted full custody of the children, regardless of the father's ability to provide emotional and practical support. In my own experience, I have seen this bias firsthand, as the mother abused the children, and despite extensive evidence, the court was initially ready to convert custody back to the mother.

It is critical to note that every case is unique, but the inequity in the family court system is a significant problem that cannot be ignored. Black fathers are just as capable of providing the love and support their children need, and it is time for society to recognize and value their contribution to the family dynamic. While there are certainly exceptions, the system often fails black fathers, leaving them to feel guilty until proven innocent.

We must recognize that black fathers face distinct difficulties that are often overlooked or disregarded, such as poverty, mass incarceration, and discriminatory family court systems. Additionally, the mothers' conscious or unconscious psychological manipulation of the child can also impact the relationship between black fathers and their children.

Just like a seed that faces many obstacles before it can sprout, black fathers face numerous challenges in their journey to be present and participating in their children's lives. But just as the seed perseveres and breaks through the soil to grow into a strong and fruitful plant, black fathers too exhibit strength and toughness in overcoming the odds and nurturing their children. We cannot let these obstacles define the image of black fatherhood, but instead, we must acknowledge and celebrate the determination and love of these fathers.

The issue of absent fathers is not unique to the black community. Fathers of all races and backgrounds struggle to maintain relationships with their children. The challenges faced by black fathers in maintaining relationships with their children can be exacerbated by failed relationships and the emotions that come with them. Fathers may feel hurt and angry with the mother for cheating or past transgression that makes dealing with the mother such emotionally impossible. Forgiveness is normally not on the table as the hurt is so pronounced and the inability for the father to move on from that pain. On the other hand, the mother may feel rejected because the father has moved on and started a new family, leading to feelings of resentment and anger. When both parents are operating from a selfish stance, it makes it very difficult and oftentimes impossible for the two sides to come together for the benefit of the children.

As human beings, it is natural to experience a range of emotions, and hurt is often part of the deal. However, it is fundamental to recognize the impact that these emotions can have on children and their relationships with their fathers. When parents are unable to cooperate and work together, it can create a toxic environment that is detrimental to the well-being of the children.

Let's acknowledge the elephant in the room: there's a pressing question that needs to be addressed: are black fathers inherently bad or is there more to the story? It's a topic that many are hesitant to approach due to its sensitive nature. However, we cannot ignore the reality of the situation. Unfortunately, the data suggests that the perception of black fathers is predominantly bleak, a consequence of the detrimental cliche, prejudiced court systems, biased media representation, and numerous accounts of black fathers who have abandoned their families.

Exhibit A - Prosecution:

1- Barack Obama was raised by his mother and grandparents after his father left to attend Harvard University. Obama has spoken openly about the importance of fathers in the lives of children and the need for societal and cultural support for fathers.

2- Oprah Winfrey was born to a teenage mother and was raised by her grandmother for much of her childhood.

Winfrey has discussed the challenges of growing up without a father figure and the importance of seeking out positive male role models.

3- Halle Berry was raised by her mother and has spoken about the impact of her father's absence on her life, including struggles with abandonment and trust issues.

4- Tyler Perry was raised by his mother and has discussed his difficult childhood, including physical abuse and homelessness. Perry has spoken about the importance of forgiveness and the role of father figures in his life.

5- Dave Chappelle was raised by his mother after his parents separated when he was a child. Chappelle has spoken about the importance of family and fatherhood in his comedy and personal life.

6- Lebron James was raised by his mother and has spoken about the impact of his absent father on his life. James has discussed his efforts to be a present and involved father to his own children.

7- Will Smith was raised by his mother and grandmother after his parents separated when he was a child. Smith has spoken about the importance of his relationship with his own father and the role of fathers in the lives of children.

8- Jay-Z was raised by his mother after his father left the family when he was a child. Jay-Z has discussed the impact of his father's absence on his life and the importance of being a present and involved father to his own children.

9- Tupac Shakur was raised by his mother and has spoken about the difficulties of growing up without a father figure. Shakur's music often reflected his experiences with fatherlessness and the struggles of young black men.

10- Alicia Keys was raised by her mother after her parents separated when she was a child. Keys has spoken about the impact of her father's absence on her life and the importance of positive male role models.

11- Mary J. Blige was raised by her mother after her father left the family when she was a child. Blige has discussed the impact of her father's absence on her life and the challenges of growing up in poverty.

12- Morgan Freeman was raised by his grandmother and has discussed the impact of his absent father on his life. Freeman has spoken about the importance of fathers in the lives of children and the need for societal support for fatherhood.

13- Kerry Washington was raised by her mother and has spoken about the impact of her father's absence on her life. Washington has discussed the importance of positive male role models and the need for cultural change in the portrayal of black fathers.

14- Jamie Foxx was raised by his mother and has spoken about the difficulties of growing up without a father figure. Foxx has discussed the importance of forgiveness and the role of fatherhood in his own life.

15- 50 Cent was raised by his mother after his father left the family when he was a child. 50 Cent has spoken about the impact of his father's absence on his life and the importance of being a present and involved father to his own children.

16- Iyanla Vanzant was raised by her mother and has spoken about the impact of her father's absence on her life. Vanzant has discussed the need for societal and cultural change in the recognition and support of fatherhood.

17- Fantasia Barrino was raised by her grandmother and has spoken about the challenges of growing up without a father figure. Barrino has discussed the importance of forgiveness and the role of family in her life.

18- Lauryn Hill was raised by her mother and has spoken about the impact of her father's absence on her life. Hill has discussed the importance of family and forgiveness in overcoming challenges.

19- Seal was born in London to a Nigerian mother and Brazilian father. His father left the family when he was still an infant. Seal has spoken about his childhood, saying that he never knew his father and that his mother struggled to make ends meet. He credits his mother with instilling in him the values of hard work and perseverance.

20- Snoop Dogg, born Calvin Cordozar Broadus Jr., was raised in Long Beach, California by his mother and stepfather. His biological father left the family when Snoop was just three months old. Snoop has talked about the impact that his father's absence had on his life and the struggles he faced growing up without a male role model.

21- Eddie Murphy, the comedian and actor, was born in Brooklyn, New York. His parents divorced when he was young and his father, who was an amateur comedian, left the family. Murphy has spoken about the impact of his father's absence on his life, saying that it made him determined to be a good father to his own children.

22- Lil Wayne, born Dwayne Michael Carter Jr., was raised in New Orleans by his mother after his father left the family when he was two years old. Lil Wayne has spoken about his relationship with his absent father, saying that he forgave him for not being there and that he has tried to be a good father to his own children.

23- Lenny Kravitz, the musician and actor, was born in New York City to a Bahamian mother and a Jewish father. His parents divorced when he was young and his father left the family. Kravitz has spoken about his childhood and the impact of his father's absence, saying that it made him determined to be a good father to his own daughter.

24- Forest Whitaker, the actor and director, was born in Texas and raised in California by his mother after his parents divorced when he was young. Whitaker has spoken about his childhood and the impact of his father's absence on his life, saying that it made him determined to be a good father to his own children.

25- Queen Latifah, born Dana Elaine Owens, was raised in New Jersey by her mother after her parents divorced when she was young. Queen Latifah has spoken about the importance of having strong women in her life, including her mother and grandmother, and the impact of her father's absence.

26- Ludacris, born Christopher Brian Bridges, was raised in Atlanta by his mother after his parents divorced when he was young. Ludacris has spoken about the importance of his mother in his life and the impact of his father's absence on his childhood.

27- Ice Cube, born O'Shea Jackson Sr., was raised in South Central Los Angeles by his mother and stepfather. His father left the family when he was young. Ice Cube has spoken about his childhood and the impact of his father's absence on his life, saying that it urged him to be a good father to his own children.

28- Rihanna, born Robyn Rihanna Fenty, was raised in Barbados by her mother after her parents divorced when she was a child. Rihanna has spoken about her childhood and the impact of her father's absence on her life, saying that it made her stronger and more independent.

29- Jada Pinkett Smith was raised in Maryland by her mother after her parents divorced when she was young. Jada has spoken about the importance of having strong women in her life and the impact of her father's absence on her childhood.

30- Tracy Morgan, the comedian and actor, was raised in Brooklyn, New York by his mother after his parents divorced when he was young. Morgan has spoken about his childhood and the impact of his father's absence on his life, saying that it influenced him to be a good father to his own children.

31- Tracy Chapman, the musician, was raised by her mother, who separated from her biological father when Chapman was just four years old. Chapman's father was a musician who would occasionally visit her during her childhood, but their relationship was strained due to his struggles with drug addiction. Chapman has been open about the impact of her absent father on her life and music, stating in an interview with The Guardian, "I think my dad's absence played a big part in my life. In the absence of someone you love, your imagination takes over." She has also credited her mother with providing her with a strong sense of independence and self-reliance.

32- Chris Rock, the comedian, was born in South Carolina and raised in Brooklyn by his mother and grandparents. His father left the family when Rock was just six years old, and he has spoken publicly about the pain and anger he felt towards his absent father. In an interview with The Guardian, Rock stated, "My father was never there, and I used to resent him for that. I used to be like, 'Why doesn't he come by?' But then you grow up and realize that maybe he didn't have anything to say."

33- Kelly Rowland, the singer and former member of Destiny's Child, was raised in Houston by her mother and with the help of her grandmother. Her father left the family when she was just seven years old, and she has spoken openly about the impact of his absence on her life. In an interview with The Guardian, Rowland stated, "It was really tough not having my dad around. My mum was everything to me, but there were times when I wished I had a father figure there." Despite her father's absence, Rowland has spoken about the positive impact that her mother and grandmother had on her life, stating, "They were both so strong and supportive, and they gave me the tools to be able to deal with whatever came my way."

34- Tyra Banks, the model and television personality, was raised in California by her mother, who separated from her biological father when Banks was just six years old. Banks has spoken openly about the pain and confusion she felt when her father left the family, stating in an interview with The Guardian, "It was really tough for me when my dad left. I remember feeling like I wasn't good enough for him to stay." Despite the challenges of growing up without a father, Banks has credited her mother with providing her with the love and support she needed to succeed, stating, "My mum was my everything. She was my dad, my mum, my best friend. She gave me the strength to believe in myself."

35- Nia Long, an actress, was raised by her mother and grandparents. She has spoken about the importance of having strong role models and support systems in her life, including her mother and grandmother.

36- Terry Crews, an actor and former football player, was raised by his mother after his father abandoned the family. He has talked about his experiences with toxic masculinity and the pressure men face to be strong and unemotional.

37- Missy Elliott, a rapper and producer, was raised by her mother after her father left the family. She has spoken about the importance of having a strong work ethic and the influence her mother had on her career.

38- Lisa Leslie, a former professional basketball player and coach, was raised by her mother after her father was murdered when she was a child. She has spoken about the impact her father's death had on her and how she used basketball as an outlet to cope.

39- Montel Williams, a television personality and former talk show host, was raised by his mother after his father abandoned the family. He has talked about the challenges he faced growing up and the importance of perseverance and hard work.

40- Toni Braxton, a singer and actress, was raised by her mother after her father left the family. She has spoken about the challenges of being a single mother herself and the importance of having a support system.

41- Ne-Yo, a singer and songwriter, was raised by his mother after his father left the family. He has spoken about the impact his mother had on his life and how he learned to be a responsible and loving father himself.

42- Tank, a singer and songwriter, was raised by his mother after his father left the family. He has spoken about the importance of being present in his children's lives and the impact his mother had on his upbringing.

43- Kenan Thompson, a comedian and actor, was raised by his mother after his father left the family. He has talked about his experiences growing up and the importance of having positive male role models in his life.

44- Tichina Arnold, an actress and singer, was raised by her mother after her father died when she was a child. She has spoken about the impact her father's death had on her and how she has worked to honor his memory through her career.

45- Serena Williams and Venus Williams, professional tennis players, were raised by their mother after their father left the family. They have spoken about the importance of family and the impact their mother had on their athletic careers.

46- Regina King, an actress and director, was raised by her mother after her father left the family. She has spoken about the challenges she faced growing up and the impact her mother had on her life and career.

47- Derek Jeter, a former professional baseball player, was raised by his mother and grandmother after his father left the family. He has spoken about the importance of family and the impact his mother had on his life and career.

48- Gabrielle Union, an actress and author, was raised by her mother after her father left the family. She has spoken about her experiences with domestic violence and the importance of supporting and empowering survivors.

49- Michael Jordan, a former professional basketball player and businessman, was raised by his mother after his father was murdered when he was a teenager. He has spoken about the impact his father's death had on him and how he has used basketball as a way to honor his father's memory.

50- Shaquille O'Neal: The retired NBA star was raised by his mother and stepfather in Newark, New Jersey. He has been open about his difficult upbringing, including poverty and the loss of his biological father. In an interview with Oprah Winfrey, O'Neal discussed how he felt abandoned by his father but found a father figure in his stepfather. He also spoke about the importance of being present in his own children's lives, saying, "My kids are everything to me.

They're my jewels. They're my legacy. When I'm gone, they'll be the ones carrying on the O'Neal name."

The issue of absent black fathers is a contentious one, with discouraging reactions often accompanying any discussion of the topic. The stories of 50 famous individuals who were raised without their biological fathers, as well as countless ordinary children who lack the ability to tell their own stories, have only added fuel to this fire. It is important to avoid lumping all black fathers into one troubling designation and instead recognize that each person's individual circumstances and experiences shape their parenting outcomes. However, the widespread familiarity with these celebrities' stories makes it easy for harmful predispositions and stigma to be spread and maintained, further isolating the black image in America.

On the other hand, these stories also serve as a testament to the fortitude of black children who rise above their circumstances and become successful, even without their biological fathers. In this volume, I aim to shed light on the potential of black children who grow up without their fathers. Despite the absence of a biological father figure, these children can still rise like a phoenix from the ashes and become successful in their own right. My hope is that this book can be a beacon of light for those who may have grown up without their fathers and inspire them to become great parents themselves, breaking the cycle of abandonment. I urge readers to approach this topic with an open mind and heart, recognizing that life is full of gray areas and that forgiveness and understanding can pave the way for a life that is both harmonious and satisfying.

The issue of absent fathers in America is a complex one, and it goes beyond the individual circumstances of each family. It is a problem that affects society as a whole, leading to higher crime rates, a breakdown in social order, and the perpetuation of distressing conventions. The impact of absent fathers is felt most acutely by children, who are left to navigate the world without the guidance and support of a parent. This can lead to feelings of abandonment, insecurity, and a lack of self-esteem that can have comprehensive consequences.

Unfortunately, black fathers in America face unmatched tests that make it even more difficult for them to be present in their children's lives. These challenges include discrimination in the criminal justice system, lack of access to education and employment opportunities, and the disappointing portrayals continuously propagated by the media. These obstacles can lead to a sense of hopelessness and defeat that make it difficult for black fathers to be committed to their children's well-being.

But there is hope! We can recognize the vital role that fathers play in the lives of their children, and by working to break down the hindrances that make it difficult for black fathers to be present and engaged, we can create a brighter future for all children and families. This means advocating for fair custody arrangements in family court, providing support for fathers who want to be involved in their children's lives, and celebrating the positive impact that fathers can have on their children's development.

The shackles of the past are weighing down on black families in America; the chains of prejudices and biases have been holding black fathers back for far too long, slowly eroding the fabric of our association. We must now realize the significance of fatherhood and actively support all fathers in their journey towards becoming the best possible parents they can be. It is vital to note that the struggle of black families in America is not merely anecdotal, but rather backed by statistics and data. According to a report by the National Center for Health Statistics, over 70% of black children are born to unwed mothers. Additionally, the fatherlessness rate among black families is significantly higher than any other racial group, with nearly 2 out of 3 black children growing up in households without their biological fathers. This trend is also reflected in poverty rates, as nearly 50% of black children live in poverty, with fatherlessness being a key factor in perpetuating this cycle. We can create a better future for our children by promoting positive fatherhood and breaking the cycle of poverty and fatherlessness in black families, thus defying the negative statistics and data that often plague our population.

CHAPTER TWO

Statistics and Data on Black Families

T he historical disparities in marriage rates between Black and white Americans are an undeniable reality. The reasons for this disparity are multidimensional, and can be traced back to a long history of racial inequality and discrimination. Before the civil rights movement, marriage rates among Black Americans were significantly lower than those of white Americans, with only 50% of Black Americans being married in 1950. Moreover, the marriage gap between Black and white Americans was even greater for women, with only 38% of Black women being married compared to 66% of white women.

The civil rights movement was a social and political movement in the United States that fought for equal rights and fair treatment for Black Americans. The civil rights movement stands as an epic and indelible testament to the unflinching courage, unyielding determination, and unwavering spirit of those who fought for equal rights and fair treatment for African Americans in the United States. Emerging from the tumultuous social and political landscape of the 1950s, the civil rights movement was a bold and audacious attempt to challenge the suffocating grip of discrimination, segregation, and violence that had long stigmatized and oppressed the Black community in virtually every aspect of life, including education, housing, employment, and voting.

Using a potent and multidimensional approach, the civil rights movement leveraged the power of nonviolent protests, civil disobedience, and legal challenges to wage a relentless war against these entrenched injustices and demand meaningful change. Spearheaded by an array of towering figures, including Martin Luther King Jr., Rosa Parks, and Malcolm X, the movement inspired millions of people to take action and stand up for their rights.

Through the sheer force of their unshakable will, unbridled passion, and steely resolve, the civil rights movement triumphed over adversity and injustice, paving the way for a brighter, more equitable future for millions of Black Americans. And though the road ahead remained fraught with obstacles and challenges, the movement's enduring legacy and profound impact on American society can still be felt to this day, as evidenced by the passage of laws that banned discrimination and protected the civil rights of all people, regardless of their race.

Following the civil rights movement, the marriage rates among Black Americans started to improve, and the gap between Black and white Americans began to narrow in the 1970s. However, despite these gains, the marriage rate among Black Americans remained lower than that of white Americans. The impact of this disparity on the Black community cannot be overstated, as marriage is a crucial institution that has a significant impact on the well-being of individuals and families.

In recent years, there has been a decline in marriage rates among all Americans, but the decline has been more pronounced among Black Americans. According to data from the Pew Research Center, in 2019, only 30% of Black adults ages 18 and older were married, compared to 56% of white adults. This is a significant disparity that must be addressed, as it has long-term implications for the well-being of the Black experience. The reasons for this decline in marriage rates are complex, and cannot be attributed to any one factor. However, it is clear that addressing this issue will require a multi-pronged approach that takes into account the rare predicaments faced by Black Americans.

The decline in marriage rates among Black Americans is a complex issue with a variety of contributing factors. One major factor is economic inequality, as Black Americans often have limited access to stable jobs and affordable housing. This lack of stability can make it difficult for Black Americans to form and maintain healthy relationships, including marriage. Additionally, the legacy of systemic racism, which has created limitations to educational and economic opportunities for Black Americans, can also play a role in the decline of marriage rates.

Statistics on black fatherhood show concerning trends, with many black fathers living apart from their children. The

National Fatherhood Initiative reports that a high percentage of black children are born to unmarried parents. However, these statistics do not necessarily mean that black fathers are absent or uninvolved in their children's lives. In fact, research shows that black fathers are just as committed to their children's lives as fathers of other races.

A study published in the Journal of Marriage and Family found that black fathers are more likely to engage in physical play with their children than white fathers. This highlights the importance of paternal involvement in child advancement. Another study published in the Journal of Family Issues showed that black fathers are more likely than fathers of other races to provide emotional support to their children. This suggests that black fathers are not only present in their children's lives but are also actively engaged in nurturing and supporting them.

The importance of fathers in the household is often underestimated, especially when it comes to the black neighborhood. However, several case studies highlight the positive impact that involved black fathers can have on their children and themselves. For instance, the Institute for Family Studies conducted a study which states that when black fathers are involved in their children's lives, they are more likely to experience greater job satisfaction and less likely to experience depression. This highlights the important role that fathers play in providing emotional support and stability in the household. Moreover, the same study found that children who have involved black fathers have better academic outcomes, higher self-esteem, and fewer behavioral problems. This emphasizes the crucial role that fathers play in their children's maturation and success.

In addition, a study published in the American Journal of Community Psychology found that black fathers who participate in community-based programs designed to support them in their parenting roles have better mental health outcomes and are more likely to stay involved in their children's lives. This highlights the importance of providing resources and support for black fathers to help them guide the challenges of fatherhood and be present and invested in their children's development.

Here are some illuminating studies that investigate the impact of fathers in the household compared to their absence, providing a fascinating read.

McLanahan, S., & Sandefur, G. (1994). Growing Up With a Single Parent: What Hurts, What Helps. Harvard University Press:

In "Growing Up With a Single Parent: What Hurts, What Helps," authors Sara McLanahan and Gary Sandefur paint a vivid picture of the challenges faced by children growing up without both parents present in the household. Through their research, they reveal the stark statistics that highlight the disheartening outcomes often associated with single-parent families, such as a higher likelihood of poverty, lower educational attainment, and increased risk of behavioral and emotional problems. However, they also offer hope, exploring ways in which single-parent families can still thrive and succeed with the right support and resources. McLanahan and Sandefur's work serves as a powerful reminder of the importance of positive fatherhood and the need for a concerted effort to break the cycle of fatherlessness in black families.

Flouri, E., & Buchanan, A. (2003). The role of father involvement in children's later mental health. Journal of Adolescence, 26(1), 63–78:

In the study conducted by Flouri and Buchanan (2003), they explored the impact of father involvement on children's mental health later in life. They discovered that just like a sturdy foundation for a house, a positive father-child relationship provides a strong base for a child's mental well-being as they grow older. The absence of such a relationship, on the other hand, can lead to instability and insecurity, similar to a house built on a shaky foundation. Through their research, Flouri and Buchanan painted a vivid image of the crucial role that fathers play in their children's lives.

Sroufe, L. A., Egeland, B., Carlson, E. A., & Collins, W. A. (2009). The Development of the Person: The Minnesota Study of Risk and Adaptation from Birth to Adulthood. Guilford Press:

This study is like a journey through the life of individuals, from birth to adulthood, exploring the different risks and adaptations they face along the way. It takes a deep dive into the development of the person, shedding light on the impact of childhood experiences on adult outcomes. The study focuses on the interplay between environmental and genetic factors, providing a comprehensive understanding of how both nature and nurture shape an individual's life. Through their research, Sroufe, Egeland, Carlson, and Collins provide valuable insights into how early experiences, relationships, and environments can affect a person's mental and physical health, as well as their ability to form healthy relationships and achieve success in adulthood. Their findings have significant implications for the fields of psychology, social work, and public policy, as they underscore the importance of early intervention and support for children and families facing risk factors such as poverty, abuse, and neglect. The Minnesota Study of Risk and Adaptation is a landmark study that has contributed greatly to our understanding of human development and resilience.

The role of fathers in the household cannot be underestimated, as numerous studies have highlighted the positive impact of their involvement in their children's lives. From mental health to academic outcomes, fathers can have a profound influence on their children's overall progression. Conversely, the absence of fathers in the home has been linked to a range of bleak consequences, such as increased risk of mental health issues and engagement in risky behaviors.

Like a puzzle with missing pieces, a child's life without their father can never be complete. To fill that gap, we must acknowledge the irreplaceable role that fathers play in their children's lives and provide them with the necessary resources and support to stay present. This is not just beneficial for the children and families, but also for the society as a whole. The topic of fathers in the household should be treated with the same urgency and importance as a crumbling bridge, requiring immediate attention and action.

CHAPTER THREE

The Black Family on Trial: How the US Government is to Blame

T he Black nuclear family, a unit composed of a husband, wife, and their children, is deeply rooted in the history of the United States. Despite the many hurdles that this family structure has faced over the years, the emergence of government programs designed to combat poverty has significantly influenced the Black nuclear family. This chapter will explore into the definition and historical context of the Black nuclear family, as well as the effects of government programs on its structure.

The Black nuclear family is a family structure that comprises a married couple and their children, with the father acting as the primary breadwinner and the mother serving as the primary caregiver. This family model has been a fundamental component of Black culture and society for many generations, offering a foundation of stability and assistance for both children and adults.

The Black nuclear family, much like a sturdy oak tree, has weathered the storms of history, withstanding the onslaught of adversity and hardship. This family structure, with its roots deeply embedded in Black culture and association, has stood as a symbol of hope and endurance for generations. It is a testament to the power of love and the human spirit, and has served as a beacon of light in times of darkness.

Throughout the long and complex history of the United States, the Black nuclear family has faced challenges and obstacles that would have torn apart lesser families. The horrors of slavery, the devastating impact of Jim Crow laws, and the insidious nature of systemic racism have all conspired to undermine the family structure. But in spite of these challenges, the Black nuclear family has remained a source of strength and support for its members, providing a sense of belonging and purpose in a world that often seems hostile and indifferent.

As a reminder, Jim Crow Laws were a set of laws that enforced racial segregation and discrimination against Black Americans in the United States from the late 1800s to the mid-1960s. These laws separated public places like schools, transportation, and restaurants into two sections: "whites only" and "colored." The "colored" section was often inferior and discriminated against Black people. Also, Black people were prohibited from sitting in the front of the public bus and were forced to use the back sections in the back of the bus, which were designated as "Colored".

The Jim Crow Laws also limited voting rights, education, job opportunities, and even who Black Americans could marry. These laws were enforced with violence, intimidation, and legal punishment, causing immense harm to Black Americans.

The Jim Crow system began to end in the mid-20th century due to the efforts of civil rights leaders and the Supreme Court decision in Brown v. Board of Education. Although the Jim Crow Laws are no longer in effect, their legacy of discrimination and inequality continues to impact American society today. It's important to continue working towards equality and justice for all.

Beginning in the 1960s, the United States government launched a series of programs aimed at alleviating poverty and addressing economic inequality, known as the War on Poverty. The War on Poverty was launched in the 1960s by President Lyndon B. Johnson, with the goal of reducing poverty and promoting economic opportunity. The government implemented a range of programs, including food stamps, Medicaid, and Head Start, to support low-income families. The impact of government programs on the Black nuclear family has been both positive and troubling. While these programs provided much-needed assistance to millions of Americans, they also had unintended consequences on the Black nuclear family.

One of the most significant impacts of government programs has been the erosion of the traditional roles of the father and mother within the Black nuclear family. Financial assistance and other resources provided by the government to single-parent households have greatly diminished the role of fathers as primary breadwinners. This has resulted in a breakdown of the family structure, with an increasing number of families being led by single mothers. Consequently, black mothers have started referring to themselves as "strong black women" and claiming "I can do bad by myself," and with added support from the government, some argue that black mothers have been emboldened to take a more unilateral role in society.

However, we must remember that every individual has a unique story to tell, and every situation is different. We cannot simply paint all black mothers with the same brush or make a generalization about any group for that matter. Black mothers are as diverse as mothers of any other race or ethnicity. We must recognize that while some black mothers have chosen to take government aid over mending relationships with fathers, this is not applicable in all cases.

Moreover, it is crucial to acknowledge that some women may not be able to stay in abusive relationships out of fear for themselves and their children. We must approach these complex issues with compassion and understanding, recognizing that each family has their own set of circumstances and challenges.

The incentivization of single parenthood, while well-intentioned, has created a situation where mothers are more likely to receive financial assistance and other benefits if they are the sole provider for their children. The focus on single mothers in government programs has created an unintended incentive for mothers to remain single, as they are more likely to receive financial assistance and other benefits if they are the sole provider for their children. This has contributed to the breakdown of the Black nuclear family and the rise of single-parent households in America. While single mothers are undoubtedly doing the best they can to provide for their children, they cannot be expected to replace the role of a father in a child's life.

Another unintended consequence of government programs focused on supporting single mothers has been the rise of absentee fathers. When the government provides financial assistance to single mothers, fathers may feel that their financial support is not necessary, leading to the breakdown of the traditional family structure. This can result in children growing up without the presence of their fathers, which can have a poor impact on their mental and emotional health.

The impact of government programs on the traditional roles of fathers and mothers in the Black nuclear family is a topic of great concern for many fathers. For James, a single father, the financial assistance provided by the government to single mothers has had unintended consequences for his family. He says, "When the government provides financial assistance to single mothers, it can make fathers feel like their role as a provider is not needed. It can erode our sense of responsibility towards our families, leaving our children without a positive male role model."

Similarly, Charles, a father of two, has experienced the impact of absentee fathers firsthand. He says, "Growing up, my father wasn't around much. It was difficult for me and my siblings to navigate life without his guidance and support. I don't want my children to have the same experience." Charles believes that government programs should focus on supporting families as a whole, rather than just single mothers. He adds, "Fathers are just as important as mothers in raising healthy and happy children. We need to create policies and programs that recognize this and support families in a comprehensive way."

For many fathers like James and Charles, the erosion of traditional family roles has led to a sense of loss and confusion for their children. Children growing up without the presence of their fathers may struggle with issues of identity and self-esteem, impacting their overall well-being and success in life. The impact of absentee fathers is vital. Children who grow up without a father in their lives are more likely to experience unfortunate outcomes such as poverty, poor academic performance, and emotional and behavioral problems. Furthermore, the breakdown of the Black nuclear family has contributed to higher rates of crime, poverty, and social instability, ultimately affecting the entire community. The absence of fathers in the municipality can lead to a lack of positive male role model examples and can contribute to a cycle of poverty and social instability and may increase the likelihood of engaging in risky behaviors or criminal activities. Therefore, the role of a father in a child's life is critical, providing emotional support, guidance, and a sense of stability.

The criticisms of government programs aimed at supporting low-income families are diverse and intricate. Some argue that these programs sustain a cycle of poverty and dependence, failing to provide long-term solutions for families in need. On the other hand, others argue that the lack of incentives for fathers to remain present in their children's lives has resulted in absentee fathers, further eroding the traditional family structure.

For black mothers like Keisha, the absence of fathers has had a substantial effect on their families. She says, "As a single mother, it's tough to provide for my children and give them the support they need without a partner. It can be a struggle to make ends meet, and it's hard to be both a mother and a father." For Keisha and many other black mothers, the lack of support from fathers can create a sense of isolation and vulnerability.

Alternative solutions to government programs must be explored to address the breakdown of the Black nuclear family. Family and fellowship support, promoting stable two-parent households, and providing education and job training programs are all important factors in promoting healthy family structures.

Reforming government programs to encourage father involvement and promote stable two-parent households is crucial. This includes addressing the incentives for single parenthood and systemic racism and discrimination. Implementing community-based solutions and addressing the root causes of poverty and inequality are also important components of reform.

Government programs aimed at alleviating poverty must take into account the importance of the father's role within the Black nuclear family. Rather than incentivizing single parenthood, these programs should focus on promoting healthy co-parenting relationships and communication between fathers and mothers. This can be achieved through family counseling, mediation services, and other resources that encourage parents to work together for the benefit of their children.

In light of the government's provision of aid to single-parent households, it would be wise to gather information about the father and their relationship with the child through a questionnaire. However, relying solely on information provided by the mother may not always provide the full picture. Thus, it may be necessary for the government to require communication with the father or provide an outlet for the father and child to speak or meet. Through this approach, the government can take a more active role in facilitating communication and potentially reuniting fathers with their children. This would go beyond financial assistance and prioritize the well-being of the family as a whole. By serving as an intermediary, the government can help bridge the gap between fathers and their children and encourage fathers to take a more active role in their children's lives. In the end, this would not only benefit individual families but also contribute to a stronger and more cohesive society.

As previously discussed, the Black nuclear family has encountered numerous obstacles in the United States, including the erosion of traditional family roles. Nonetheless, it is crucial to acknowledge that there are examples of successful co-parenting relationships, even after divorce or separation, that exist among both public figures and ordinary individuals.

Rapper Ludacris and his ex-girlfriend Tamika Fuller have been praised for their successful co-parenting relationship, despite a contentious custody battle. By prioritizing their daughter's needs and working together, they have shown a remarkable level of maturity and cooperation. Even after Ludacris initially won primary custody, they came together as a united front to co-parent their daughter and have been seen attending events together as a family. Their case study serves as an inspiration to other parents going through similar challenges and highlights the importance of effective communication, cooperation, and putting the child's best interests first.

The co-parenting relationship between NBA star Dwyane Wade and his ex-wife Siohvaughn Funches has been rife with challenges, including a bitter custody battle. Despite the difficult legal dispute, both parents have made a conscious effort to prioritize their children's needs and work together to create a stable and supportive environment for them. Wade has spoken openly about the importance of co-parenting and putting his children first, stating that "it's all about the kids." Funches, too, has expressed her commitment to co-parenting and creating a positive environment for their children, saying that "we both love our children more than anything in this world." Despite their differences, they have both remained involved in their children's lives, attending events together and sharing parenting responsibilities. In fact, Wade has even taken on a fatherly role with Funches' daughter from a previous relationship, demonstrating a level of compassion and care that is rare in co-parenting relationships. Their case study serves as an inspiring example of effective co-parenting in the face of challenges, highlighting the importance of putting the children's needs first and working together to create a positive environment for them.

The co-parenting relationship between Usher and Tameka Foster has been riddled with challenges, including a tumultuous divorce and custody battle. However, both parents have demonstrated a commitment to putting their differences aside and working together to co-parent their two children. Usher has spoken openly about the importance of co-parenting and the need to prioritize the children's needs, saying that "there's no way you can be a great parent and not be there." Foster has similarly expressed her commitment to co-parenting and creating a positive environment for their children, stating that "I just try to focus on being the best mother that I can be." Despite their challenges, Usher and Foster have been seen attending events together as a family and sharing parenting responsibilities. Their successful co-parenting relationship serves as an inspiring example of the power of putting the children's needs first and working together to create a positive environment for them, even in the face of challenges.

Another inspirational example is the story of Swizz Beatz and Mashonda Tifrere: This former couple has successfully co-parent their son since their divorce in 2010. They have remained committed to co-parenting their son and prioritizing his well-being above their personal differences. They have been seen attending events and activities together with their son, and even vacationing together as a family. Tifrere has spoken publicly about the importance of co-parenting and the need to put the children first, stating that "We have to create a bond so that our child understands that we're both in his corner." Beatz has similarly emphasized the importance of effective communication and working together, saying that "It's about being mature and putting the kids first." Their successful co-parenting relationship serves as an inspiring example of the power of effective communication, cooperation, and putting the children's needs first, even after a difficult divorce.

The case studies mentioned above demonstrate that Black parents are capable of successfully co-parenting their children even after divorce or separation. Moreover, there are countless other examples of regular Black parents who have committed to co-parenting in the face of division, prioritizing the well-being of their children above all else. The decision to co-parent is not always an easy one, especially in the wake of a tumultuous separation, but these examples show that it is possible to put aside personal differences and work together for the betterment of the children. In doing so, these parents provide a source of inspiration and hope for others who may be struggling with co-parenting after divorce or separation.

Co-parenting is a choice which requires open communication, compromise, and a willingness to put the child's needs first. Since co-parenting between the parties is possible, our aim should be focused on providing government programs aimed at promoting healthy co-parenting relationships and communication with the goal of supporting the family as a whole. Through offering resources and support to both parents, these programs can help ensure that children receive the stability and support they need to thrive, even in the face of adversity.

Lastly, while the government's intention to alleviate poverty through their programs is commendable, it is clear that much-needed changes are necessary to help reduce the pain and suffering of the Black nuclear family. The evidence is clear that these programs have had unintended consequences on the traditional roles of the father and mother, resulting in the breakdown of the family structure. However, it is not too late to take action. We must come together as a society to study what works and what needs to be modified for the sake of our greatest resource: our children. Single mothers should be supported wholeheartedly, but we need to focus on supporting the whole family to ensure the best outcomes for our children. This includes promoting stable two-parent households and encouraging father involvement, implementing education and job training programs, and addressing systemic racism and discrimination. Through collaborative efforts that prioritize healthy co-parenting relationships and effective communication, we can ensure that the Black nuclear family continues to embody a symbol of hope and tenacity for generations to come.

CHAPTER FOUR

The Silent Sabotage: How a Mother's Treatment Can Shape the Image of Black Fathers

I n many ways, a mother's treatment of the father of her children is like a silent force, slowly molding and shaping the image of black fathers. This force is often hidden beneath the surface, manifesting in subtle yet powerful ways that can have a lasting impact on the father-child relationship. In this chapter, we will explore the concept of this silent sabotage and how it can sustain grim characterizations and inclinations against black fathers.

In my commitment to share my personal experiences with this topic. I remembered before my daughter turned 13, we had a close and loving relationship. However, after that age, everything changed. I received a text message from her accusing me of paying child support for my other children but not for her. The contents of that message shattered our bond and marked a turning point in our relationship. She grew distant, began giving me attitude, and even refused to come to my house. It was a painful realization of how fragile relationships can be, and how easily they can be broken with no warning or explanation. After experiencing devastation, I sought comfort from family and friends, but none could offer the right answer. They simply advised me to give my daughter time to process her emotions, hoping that she would eventually come around.

The emotional impact of a mother's treatment of the father can be overwhelming, affecting both the father and the children. The detrimental emotions can spill over onto the children, creating an environment of tension and conflict. This can lead to children feeling unloved, neglected, and abandoned by their father, even if he is doing his best to be present and supportive.

For instance, a study by the National Fatherhood Initiative found that children of unmarried parents were more likely to experience distressing emotions, such as sadness and anger, than children of married parents. The study also found that children of unmarried parents were more likely to experience behavioral problems and perform poorly in school. These dismal outcomes can be exacerbated when the mother is actively unfavorable towards the father, creating an environment of hostility and tension in the home.

For black fathers, the situation is more complicated because of societal bias and derogatory assumptions. They are often assumed to be absent or uninvolved, making it difficult for them to gain recognition and respect as caregivers. This can be demoralizing, leading to feelings of frustration, anger, and hopelessness.

A study by the American Psychological Association found that black fathers were more likely to report experiencing discrimination in their roles as caregivers than fathers of other races. These hurtful experiences can create a sense of alienation and isolation for black fathers, making it more difficult for them to maintain a strong presence in their children's lives. Moreover, research has shown that the emotional impact of a mother's unpleasant treatment of the father can have lasting effects on children's advancement. They may struggle with emotional regulation, difficulty forming healthy relationships, and poor academic performance.

A study published in the journal Development and Psychopathology found that children who experienced high levels of inter-parental conflict were more likely to struggle with emotional regulation and exhibit externalizing behaviors, such as aggression and disobedience. These painful outcomes were particularly pronounced when the conflict was frequent and intense, suggesting that even occasional pessimistic interactions between parents can have a lasting impact on children.

Little did we know that the undesirable treatment experienced by parents could have intergenerational effects. It is alarming to think that children of parents who have undergone high levels of conflict are at risk of encountering similar conflicts in their own relationships. The consequences of such experiences can be far-reaching and long-lasting, affecting not just one generation, but potentially many more to come.

For example, a study by the University of Rochester found that children of parents who experienced high levels of inter-parental conflict were more likely to exhibit harmful conflict behaviors in their own romantic relationships as young adults. These adverse conflict behaviors included yelling, criticizing, and blaming, suggesting that the emotional impact of disheartening treatment can be long-lasting and extensive.

To combat these damaging effects, it is crucial to provide support and resources to black fathers and families. This support can take many forms, including education about healthy relationship dynamics, access to counseling and mental health services, and policies that promote economic stability and equal access to opportunities.

The impact of a mother's treatment of the father is so immense that it can shake the very foundation of fathers and their children's lives. The Responsible Fatherhood Initiative and the National Healthy Marriage Resource Center are like a lifeline for fathers and families, offering a plethora of resources and support. From communication skills workshops to financial management and co-parenting, fathers are offered a wealth of knowledge and assistance. Even individual counseling and support groups are available to provide a safe haven for fathers to share their experiences and receive feedback from other fathers and professionals. Policies that promote economic stability and equal opportunities can ease the burden of stress and anxiety that can contribute to deleterious treatment and conflict in the home, and access to affordable housing, quality healthcare, and stable employment can provide the much-needed stability to reduce the economic pressures that intensify conflict and tension in the home.

The Affordable Care Act, for example, has expanded access to healthcare for millions of Americans, including black fathers and their families. By supplying access to preventive care and mental health services, it has helped reduce the financial burden of healthcare costs, reducing one potential source of stress and anxiety for families. Policies that promote access to affordable housing can help reduce financial strain and promote stability for families. The Housing Choice Voucher Program provides low-income families with vouchers that can be used to help pay for housing. This program has helped millions of families, including many headed by single parents, access safe and affordable housing, reducing the stress and instability that can contribute to harmful treatment and conflict.

Finally, policies that promote stable employment and access to education and training can help provide fathers with the tools they need to be successful caregivers and providers. Programs like the Workforce Innovation and Opportunity Act provide funding for job training and education programs, helping fathers acquire the skills and knowledge they need to access stable, well-paying jobs.

To sum up, although a mother's treatment of the father can have a profound emotional impact on the father, it is crucial for fathers to understand that this should not be a reason to give up on their children. Despite the obstacles that may arise, as research has shown that a father's presence can have a positive impact on a child's capabilities into an adult.

The author would like to emphasize that each father's circumstance is unique, and there may be situations where fathers face insurmountable barriers that make it difficult to be a consistent presence in their children's lives. Nevertheless, fathers must recognize the importance of their role as caregivers and providers and should seek support and resources to manage any challenges they may encounter.

Above all, the well-being of children should be the highest priority, and fathers should take every step possible to ensure that their children have the resources and support they need to flourish. While it may not always be easy, the author strongly encourages fathers to persist in their efforts to support their children, recognizing that the rewards of a strong and positive relationship between a father and child are immeasurable.

Personal Anecdotes and Stories

To truly grasp the experiences of black fathers, it is imperative to delve into personal anecdotes and stories that bring to light the challenges and obstacles they face on a daily basis. One black father, for instance, shared his experience of being denied custody of his child solely because of his race. Despite being a responsible and involved parent, he was informed by the court that his skin color made him less suitable to raise his child compared to his white ex-wife. This unjust and discriminatory experience left him feeling frustrated and disillusioned with the justice system. It highlighted the systemic issues that black fathers often face when seeking custody of their children, and the long-standing struggle for racial equality that continues to impact many aspects of their lives.

Similarly, another black father opened up about the challenges of co-parenting with a mother who constantly belittled and undermined him in front of their children. Despite his best efforts to be present and supportive, the mother's poor treatment created an environment of tension and conflict that made it difficult for him to maintain a strong presence in his children's lives. He found himself struggling with emotional turmoil as he tried to negotiate the complexities of the co-parenting relationship. This experience highlighted the emotional toll that grimacing treatment can have on fathers and the importance of building strong co-parenting relationships that prioritize the well-being of the children above all else.

The struggles that black fathers encounter in their efforts to be actively involved in their children's lives are numerous and complex. These previously mentioned personal anecdotes are just a few examples of the many obstacles they face. Such hurdles include systemic alienations that impede their ability to be recognized and respected as caregivers, as well as injurious treatment from mothers and other family members. Navigating these challenges can prove to be formidable and can ultimately result in difficulties in maintaining strong, healthy relationships with their children.

Nonetheless, these anecdotes also exemplify the persistence and perseverance of black fathers who are unwilling to abandon their children, even when the odds seem insurmountable. Whether it involves fighting for custody through the legal system or actively seeking out assistance and resources to manage the complexities of co-parenting, black fathers are committed to be present for their children and furnish them with the affection, guidance, and encouragement necessary for their well-being.

According to research, the influence of involved black fathers on their children's growth is akin to a superhero's impact on saving the world. A study conducted by the National Fatherhood Initiative revealed that children of engaged fathers had a significantly higher likelihood of excelling academically, displaying positive social behaviors, and experiencing greater levels of self-esteem and general life satisfaction. This research underscores the importance of providing unwavering support and resources to black fathers, who are the unsung heroes in their children's lives.

However, the personal anecdotes and stories of black fathers also reveal the numerous challenges they face in their journey to be present and supportive of their children's growth. These stories highlight the need for a more balanced and sophisticated approach to family dynamics, one that acknowledges the importance of both parents in a child's life. It is of utmost importance to recognize that every story has two versions, and fathers' versions are often not heard.

Despite any mistakes a father may have made against the mother, including remarrying or other grave errors, it is crucial to recognize the value of the father-child bond and the positive impact it can have on a child's evolution into adulthood. Children need both parents, including the mother and the father, and denying a child the opportunity to bond with their father can have long-lasting awful consequences. This is because it can lead to feelings of loneliness and insecurity, which can have a disappointing impact on the child's development.

Providing resources and support that promote positive co-parenting relationships and supporting black fathers and families can lead to the building of stronger, healthier families and communities. The benefits of this extend beyond the child's growth, as it contributes to the overall improvement of the family structure and society as a whole. The child is more likely to grow up to be a productive and engaged citizen, benefiting themselves and eventually having a positive impact in the world.

Finally, the emotional impact of how a mother treats the father, combined with the challenges that black fathers face, is nothing short of a call to action for a more comprehensive and compassionate approach to family dynamics. It is essential to recognize the irreplaceable value of both parents and the monumental role they play in a child's upbringing. By offering assistance and resources that promote positive co-parenting relationships, we can create an environment that unleashes the full potential and success of every child. And let's not forget, just as the mother's treatment of the father holds significant weight. Fathers must also steer clear of undesirable behaviors if they want to create a positive relationship with their children. This is especially important as the child's development is at stake.

Role of Anger and Revenge

When discussing family dynamics, it's important to examine how anger and revenge can negatively impact black fathers. In cases where the father is the abuser, the mother may fear for her and her children's safety and may deny the father access to the child. However, in situations where the mother is angry or resentful towards the father, it can lead to a desire for revenge or punishment. This can result in the mother using the child as a pawn to hurt the father by denying him access to the child or manipulating the child's feelings towards the father.

The devastating impact of trauma and neglect on children caught in the middle of dysfunctional family dynamics cannot be ignored. Research has shown that fatherlessness can lead to a range of bleak outcomes, including poor academic performance, behavioral problems, and mental health issues. Children who grow up without their fathers are also at higher risk of dropping out of school, getting involved in criminal activity, and struggling with substance abuse.

In the grand scheme of things, the impact of fatherlessness cannot be solely attributed to the mother's discouraging treatment towards the father. It's true that some fathers choose to abandon their responsibilities, leaving behind a trail of destruction and despair. It's as if they have no regard for the wellbeing of their own flesh and blood, and their actions only fuel a desire for revenge or punishment in the mother's heart. It's a sad reality, but not all fathers want to be involved in co-parenting, even if it means turning their backs on their own children.

Fatherlessness is a plague that not only affects individual children, but also poisons the roots of the community. It is a weed that grows in the cracks of society, choking out the potential for growth and prosperity. The absence of strong male figures can create a barren landscape where the seeds of poverty, crime, and inequality take root and flourish. The irony is that the very absence of fathers, who should provide stability and guidance, is what contributes to the sense of hopelessness and despair that pervades many communities.

Amidst the sea of societal norms and intolerance, the plight of black fathers often goes unnoticed, as they struggle to navigate through the treacherous waters of oversimplification and marginalization. It is ironic that a group that plays such a vital role in the upbringing of their children is constantly overlooked and undervalued by society. To turn the tide, we must recognize the symbol of the unrecognized father and champion their cause, breaking down the challenges that hinder their progress and promoting a system that celebrates and supports all parents in their noble quest to raise happy, healthy children.

Policies and programs that promote access to affordable housing, quality healthcare, and stable employment can help address the root causes of anger and resentment that can contribute to troubling treatment and conflict in the home. Support for positive co-parenting relationships is also essential to building stronger and healthier families.

While it is crucial to acknowledge the challenges that black fathers face, it is also important to recognize that fathers have a responsibility to make a better effort to be outstanding in their roles as caregivers and providers. Fathers need to take a more active role in co-parenting. This is not subject to negotiation!

Additionally, it is vital to address the issue of domestic violence and abuse by black men. For instance, consider the case of Rihanna, a well-known singer and actress who was the victim of domestic violence at the hands of her partner, Chris Brown. In 2009, Brown physically assaulted Rihanna in a car after an argument, leaving her with visible injuries. This incident brought attention to the issue of domestic violence against black women and highlighted the importance of holding perpetrators accountable for their actions. Despite the trauma and emotional distress caused by the assault, Rihanna spoke out about her experience and used her platform to raise awareness about the issue. Her courage and tenacity in the face of adversity serve as a powerful reminder of the need for support and resources for victims of domestic violence, particularly those in marginalized communities such as black women.

I would also like to highlight another example: In 2014, Janay Palmer, then-fiancee and now wife of NFL player Ray Rice, was knocked unconscious by Rice in an elevator at a hotel in Atlantic City. The incident was caught on camera, and Rice was later suspended by the NFL and charged with assault. The incident sparked a national conversation about domestic violence and the role of professional sports leagues in addressing the issue.

The reality of domestic violence in the black population cannot be ignored or downplayed. Countless women are subjected to physical, emotional, financial, and other forms of abuse, and this is a major issue that must be addressed. It is a must that we put an end to this cycle of violence for the betterment of our communities. Any other alternative is unacceptable and should not be considered.

The issue of single-parent households is like a tangled web, with layers of complexity that can be difficult to unravel. It's like a puzzle that requires a delicate touch to piece together. Children from these households are like seeds that need nurturing from both parents to grow and thrive, but without that support, they may struggle to take root and flourish. Society needs to dig deep to understand the root causes of this problem and plant the seeds of change to create a more equitable and just system. This may require uprooting and removing the thorny issues of poverty, discrimination, and unemployment that contribute to family breakdown and instability. It's a tall order, but a necessary one. Mothers must resist the temptation to use revenge as fertilizer for their anger towards the father, and fathers must not shy away from their responsibilities. We need to paint a different picture of black men as human beings, not just caricatures on TV and movies, to give them the opportunity to take root and bloom as fathers and as members of their communities. It's a collective effort, a call to all hands on deck, to cultivate a garden of strong and healthy families. And fathers, please step up!

CHAPTER FIVE

The Emotional Impact on Children

G rowing up without a father figure can leave a profound emotional impact on children, which can continue into the later years of life. In this chapter, we will explore the complex effects of a father's absence or neglect on children's mental and emotional health, their sense of self-worth and identity, and their relationships with others. The emotional impact of an absent or neglectful father on children is a grave issue that affects people from all walks of life. This includes celebrities who are not exempt from the emotional trauma of growing up without a father figure.

For instance, former First Lady Michelle Obama has candidly spoken about how her father's absence impacted her emotional well-being. Her father was battling multiple sclerosis, which made it difficult for him to be present in her life. She has shared how her father's absence left her feeling uncertain of herself and yearning for validation from others.

Also, actor and producer Tyler Perry grew up without a father, and has openly spoken about how his mother's love and support helped him to overcome the emotional pain of his father's absence. In an interview with Oprah Winfrey, he recounted how he had to grapple with feelings of anger and abandonment, but eventually learned to forgive his father and concentrate on the positive role models in his life.

Similarly, actress and producer Viola Davis has spoken about her own experiences growing up without a father. In an interview with People magazine, she shared how her father's absence left her feeling unlovable and insecure, and how she had to work hard to overcome these feelings as an adult.

These examples underscore the complex and profound emotional impact that absent or neglectful fathers can have on children, irrespective of their background or socio-economic status. It is crucial for parents and caregivers to recognize the significance of a father figure in a child's emotional development and provide steady emotional support and guidance to help mitigate the bad effects of a father's absence. Additionally, society must address the systemic biases and prejudiced misconceptions that contribute to the disenfranchisement of black fathers. This can be achieved through promoting positive co-parenting relationships, as well as providing access to resources and support that promote economic stability and equal access to opportunities, ultimately contributing to stronger, healthier families and communities.

Growing up without a father can leave a deep emotional impact on any child, one that often carries across the lifespan. Studies have shown that fatherless children are at a higher risk of developing emotional and behavioral problems that can be long-lasting. These problems include low self-esteem, anxiety, depression, and difficulty forming healthy relationships. Furthermore, they may also display behavioral problems such as delinquency, aggression, and substance abuse.

Unfortunately, societal stereotypes and disgrace can add to the emotional burden felt by children without a father figure. In particular, black children often face damaging portrayals in the media, perpetuating harmful caricatures and fostering social stigma. This can leave children feeling ashamed and guilty, and it can further affect their mental and emotional well-being. However, children can overcome the emotional trauma of growing up without a father figure. Positive male guides can provide the guidance and support needed to steer through life's challenges. These role models may include uncles, grandfathers, or mentors. Counseling and therapy can also be effective in helping children process and heal from the emotional pain of an absent father by learning how to develop coping mechanisms to succeed in life.

It is indispensable to address the impact of absent fathers and work towards a future where all children have access to positive male mentors and support systems. This can help to create stronger, healthier families and communities, and it can ensure that future generations do not have to suffer from the emotional toll of growing up without a father figure.

Growing up without a father figure can have a significant impact on a child's emotional and behavioral health. This lack of support may lead to problems such as increased aggression, anxiety, and depression. Children may feel abandoned and neglected, struggling to develop a sense of identity and purpose. This can lead to a host of emotional and behavioral problems, including delinquency, substance abuse, and even suicidal thoughts. As a society, it is crucial to recognize the impact of fatherlessness and work to address the root causes of this issue.

Moreover, societal profiling and stigmatization of non-traditional family structures can worsen the emotional impact on children. Media images of white families with strong father figures can be harmful and create stigma for children who don't have that family dynamic. This can lead to psychological trauma, creating feelings of isolation, inadequacy, and low self-worth. The lack of participation on the part of the father can also lead to deep resentment, anger, and emotional distress for the child.

For instance, when a child is involved in sports and only the mothers attend the games, while their peers' fathers are present, the child may feel embarrassed and ashamed, which can cause them to distance themselves from their peers. Addressing the emotional trauma that children may experience due to the absence of a father figure is crucial. Counseling and therapy can provide children with the tools and support they need to process and heal from their emotional pain.

Providing children with positive male idols and a supportive environment is essential in helping them build a strong sense of self-worth and identity, and empowering them to overcome the challenges that come with growing up without a father. Black fathers face many challenges in being present and attentive to their children's needs, but some "dads" refuse to give up on their children, despite the odds stacked against them. It is indispensable to recognize and support these fathers as they sail the challenges of fatherhood.

It is of utmost importance that we take action to prevent our children from growing up with emotional trauma that could potentially result in them becoming hurt parents themselves. This is a devastating phenomenon that we must strive to avoid at all costs. Unfortunately, the reality is that many children are struggling with emotional distress and do not have access to the proper resources to help them cope. According to a study by the National Fatherhood Initiative, children who grow up without a father are four times more likely to live in poverty, and are at a higher risk of experiencing emotional and behavioral problems. It is crucial that we recognize the importance of a father figure in a child's life and provide the necessary support to help mitigate the sorrowful effects of an absent or neglectful father. Additionally, we must listen to the stories of those who have experienced the impact of an absent or neglectful father firsthand, such as author Ta-Nehisi Coates, who has written about his own struggles with his father's absence and the emotional toll it took on his life. Only by recognizing and addressing these issues can we work towards building a healthier and more equitable society for our children.

Personal Stories from Children

Growing up without a father figure can have a profound impact on a child's emotional well-being, and personal stories from children who have experienced this first-hand can provide valuable insight into the unique challenges they face.

One child shared a story about growing up with an absent father, saying, "My dad left when I was young, and I didn't understand why. I felt like I was the reason he left, and that made me feel unlovable." This child struggled with low self-esteem and difficulty forming healthy relationships due to the feelings of abandonment and neglect they experienced.

Another child spoke about the challenges of growing up without a father figure, stating, "I never had anyone to teach me how to be a man. I felt like I had to figure everything out on my own, and that was really hard." This child struggled with forming a sense of identity and purpose due to the lack of guidance and support from a male figure in his life.

Another child shared a story about growing up with a neglectful father, saying, "My dad was there, but he wasn't really present. He didn't show up to my school events or spend time with me. It made me feel like I wasn't important to him." This child struggled with feelings of rejection and loneliness, as well as difficulty forming healthy relationships due to the lack of attention and care he received from his father.

Like a garden deprived of sunlight, each tale illuminates the emotional landscape of children navigating life without the warmth of a father figure. They weather storms of self-doubt and identity, their roots seeking stable ground for nurturing connections. Yet, with a gentle touch of guidance and sustenance, these tender saplings reveal their innate resilience, blossoming triumphantly through adversity. The weight of fatherlessness casts a long shadow over the hearts of children, an issue demanding attention. As the sun rises on the horizon, counseling and therapy emerge as beacons of hope, guiding young souls through the healing process. Yet, a subtle darkness looms, for not all children can bask in the warm embrace of these resources. Without the necessary support, they risk stumbling through a tangled web of emotions and behaviors, the effects of which may echo into the distant halls of adulthood.

Personal stories from children who have grown up without a father provide a glimpse into the immense emotional impact of fatherlessness. These stories are heartbreaking and reveal the devastating consequences that can result from growing up without a father. Children may experience feelings of abandonment, rejection, and loneliness, which can lead to a range of emotional and behavioral problems, rage and any hoax of unexplained psychological issues.

In the quiet corners of a child's heart, unspoken frustrations and bottled emotions may take root, entwining their tendrils around the fragile core of their being. As the shadow of this silent struggle stretches into the future, whispers of cycles unbroken and dysfunction perpetuated become more evident. With each passing generation, the specter of fatherlessness looms larger, indiscriminately casting its pall over children of all backgrounds. It is in the shared vulnerability of our humanity that we find a common thread, binding us together in our quest to break free from the chains of history.

As someone who had the privilege of growing up with a father in the household, I cannot imagine the pain and trauma that children who grow up without a father must endure. It is essential that we recognize the importance of fatherhood and work towards creating a society that provides the resources and support necessary to help children handle the challenges they may face as a result of fatherlessness. On the other side of the coin, the lack of guidance can lead some children down a path of gangs, juvenile delinquency, and other unfavorable outcomes that certainly don't benefit society. As we look toward the future, it's important to acknowledge this possibility and work together to prevent it, ensuring a brighter and more promising legacy for everyone.

Positive male role models can play a significant role in supporting children and helping them to develop a healthy relationship with the male figures in their lives. These influencers can provide guidance, support, and a positive influence, helping children govern the challenges they may face as a result of fatherlessness.

As a society, it is our responsibility to recognize the importance of fatherhood and work towards creating a society that provides the resources and support necessary to help children thrive, regardless of their family structure. Counseling and therapy, along with positive male teachers, can provide children with the tools and support they need to build healthy relationships and a positive sense of self-worth.

As the final pages of this chapter turn, we find ourselves at a crossroads where the fate of generations hangs in the balance. This tale is not only of families of color, but rather a human story that entwines the lives of children across the vast tapestry of race and ethnicity. This story is not only about families of color, but it is also a human story that intertwines the lives of children from all different ethnicities. With the whispers of tomorrow urging us to act, we must rise to the challenge and write a new narrative, one where we nurture and uplift the hearts of our children, ensuring a brighter future for all.

Role of Mothers in the Emotional Well-being of Children

Mothers are often tasked with helping their children manage the emotional complexities of growing up without a father figure. It can be a difficult balancing act, as mothers must simultaneously acknowledge the absence of the father while also providing their child with a sense of love and support. One mother shared her approach to this challenge, saying "I tell my son that his dad loves him, even if he can't be here right now. It's not his fault and it's not his dad's fault either." This approach can help children to develop a positive perspective about their fathers, even when they are not present in their lives.

Single motherhood presents its own unique set of challenges, particularly when it comes to financial stability and accessing resources. Studies have shown that single mothers are more likely to experience poverty, housing insecurity, and difficulty in accessing healthcare and childcare. The stigma associated with single motherhood can also contribute to feelings of isolation and inadequacy.

In the face of adversity, single mothers stand tall, their strength and resourcefulness wrapping around them like a protective cloak. They reach out to the nurturing embrace of community resources and support groups, finding solace in the shared warmth of collective strength. Yet, as they dance between the roles of caregiver and breadwinner, the specter of stress and anxiety casts its shadow, waiting to ensnare them in its tight grasp. A study whispers cautionary tales of heightened stress for these mothers, a burden they bear as both nurturer and provider. This ever-present shadow threatens to seep into the lives of mother and child alike, leaving its mark on their emotional well-being.

Single mothers face a myriad of challenges, ranging from emotional to financial and logistical, as they maneuver the demands of raising a child without the support of a partner. Policies that support these mothers can make a significant difference in their well-being and that of their children.

Access to affordable childcare, healthcare, and housing, as well as job training and education programs, can provide single mothers with the tools they need to secure stable and well-paying employment. However, government aid programs can create a catch-22 situation for single mothers, as benefits often require that the father is not present in the household, limiting opportunities for these families.

In the garden of our society, each family is a distinct flower, with single mothers blossoming amidst this colorful array. As we tend to these unique blooms, we must cultivate a nurturing environment that allows every family to flourish, regardless of their structure. By sowing the seeds of well-being and prioritizing the health of our children and families, we can foster a vibrant and balanced garden that cherishes the beauty and significance of each and every blossom, including those nurtured by the loving hands of single mothers.

In the intricate tapestry of our society, single mothers and their children are interwoven threads that hold the fabric together. When these threads fray under the pressures of emotional and financial stress, the delicate balance of the entire tapestry is at risk, impacting the emotional and educational flourishing of the children. Fortifying these vital threads with resources and support, we have the power to mend the tapestry and allow every child the chance to shine brightly and reach their full potential. Now is the moment for us to weave a more inclusive and caring society that values and cherishes all families, including those with single mothers at the helm.

Healing and Reconciliation

In the vast landscape of childhood, many young souls wander without the guiding compass of outlets like sports to channel their inner turmoil. As they roam, their bottled-up energy and frustration seek alternative paths, turning into destructive storms that wreak havoc on their surroundings— siblings, and even themselves. These tempests grow stronger and more ferocious over time, evolving into a cycle of violence that casts a heavy shadow across the nation. Recognizing and addressing this pressing issue is essential to changing the course and steering our youth towards a brighter horizon.

The mighty oak of fatherhood stretches its branches, casting a protective canopy over the tender saplings of childhood. Fathers, the roots of these majestic trees, offer vital emotional and financial sustenance that nourishes the growth and well-being of their offspring. Yet, for black fathers, brambles and thorns weave a complex web of obstacles, hindering their journey towards being present and dedicated to parenting their children. The tangled undergrowth of societal bias, economic challenges, and systemic issues disproportionately entangle black communities, demanding a collective effort to clear the path and let the oaks of fatherhood stand tall and proud.

A heavy cloud of misperceptions looms over black fathers, casting shadows that obscure their true presence and involvement in their children's lives. This veil, created by society, the media, and the criminal justice system, sustains the labeling of their absence or disengagement. Underneath this shroud, black fathers struggle to be recognized and respected as the caring pillars they are. The weight of these unjust assumptions erodes their spirits, sowing seeds of frustration, anger, and hopelessness. It is time we dispelled the darkness of these prejudices; we can now allow the light of truth to shine through and uplift the hearts of black fathers.

In addition, economic instability poses a significant obstacle for black fathers who aspire to be present and involved in their children's lives. The financial challenges faced by many black fathers can hinder their ability to provide for their children and maintain a stable living situation, creating additional stress and anxiety that may contribute to poor family dynamics and conflicts in the home.

Furthermore, numerous case studies have shown the crucial role that supporting black fathers can play in their roles as caregivers and providers. Growing up without a father can be emotionally devastating for children. Studies have found that the emotional impact of absent or neglectful fathers can lead to a host of emotional and behavioral issues, including depression, anxiety, and other emotional disorders. The absence of a father can also impact a child's social improvement, making it difficult for them to form healthy relationships and to trust others.

The media's portrayal of black children as coming from broken homes or having absent fathers sustains distressing preconceptions and stigmatizes them, leading to feelings of shame and guilt and ultimately impacting their ability to form healthy relationships later in life.

In the tapestry of childhood, mothers are the golden threads that intertwine, weaving a comforting blanket of emotional support around their children. When the fabric is torn by the absence or neglect of fathers, these threads become even more essential, binding the frayed edges and nurturing resilience and coping skills in their young ones. Like skilled weavers, mothers also interlace connections with other adult figures, such as male mentors, incorporating them into the pattern to provide positive role models for their children. In doing so, they ensure that the tapestry remains strong and vibrant, even when confronted with the challenges of fatherlessness.

The path of a single mother winds through treacherous terrain, strewn with obstacles that threaten to trip her at every turn. Relying on the support of government programs, like food stamps and Section 8 housing, she traverses rocky terrain, fraught with uncertainty and doubt. Though these resources offer a lifeline, the journey of accessing and maintaining them can be an uphill battle, adding to the already heavy burden of single parenthood. Another hurdle, like a jagged boulder, is the scarcity of affordable childcare, making it challenging for single mothers to work and provide for their families. Nevertheless, these brave mothers press on, resolute in their determination to overcome every obstacle and provide a better life for their children.

In the sea of society, single mothers often find themselves battered by the waves of discrimination and stigma. These waves crash against the shores of their lives, causing ripples that affect every aspect of their existence. The turbulent waters of discrimination can erode their ability to find employment, housing, and other vital resources, amplifying the obstacles they already face. This constant assault can create a whirlpool of physical, emotional, and financial strain, dragging them down into the depths of despair. Yet, like mermaids rising from the depths, these courageous mothers continue to swim against the tide, defying the currents of discrimination and stigma to provide a brighter future for themselves and their children.

Like the mightiest of trees, single mothers weather the storms of life, bending but never breaking under the weight of the challenges they face. With the support of family and friends, they anchor themselves deep in the soil of the community, tapping into its strength to grow strong and sturdy. They join support groups, like branches interweaving, to form a canopy of emotional and practical support. Their voices, like leaves rustling in the wind, advocate for policies that uplift single-parent families, nourishing the roots of their strength. Despite the harsh winds that buffet them, these mothers stand tall, resolute in their determination to provide for and support their children, like beacons of hope shining bright in the darkness.

The issue of absent and neglectful fathers is like a puzzle with many pieces, each one unique and intricate. To solve it, we must approach it with a careful handling, weaving together different strategies and resources to create a tapestry of healing and reconciliation. Like a skilled tailor, we must tailor solutions to fit the individual needs of fathers, mothers, and children, creating a garment of hope that fits perfectly. With patience and perseverance, we can assemble the puzzle piece by piece, until we see the full picture of healthy and thriving families.

Fathers, mothers, and children who are dealing with the issue of absent and neglectful fathers have access to several approaches and tools that can help them navigate these challenges and work towards restoration and forgiveness. One such effective strategy is for fathers to take responsibility for their past actions and make a commitment to being present and present for their children. This may involve seeking therapy or counseling to work through their emotions and develop strategies for repairing their relationships with their children. Additionally, fathers can seek out support from family and friends, join support groups, and advocate for policies that support fatherhood and parental involvement.

Children who have grown up without a father may benefit from seeking therapy or counseling with a trained mental health professional, as it can provide a safe space to process their experiences and feelings. They can also benefit from joining support groups and peer networks, which can provide valuable information and resources, as well as a way to connect with other children who have gone through similar experiences. Positive leaders and mentors can also provide guidance and support in navigating the challenges of growing up with an absent or neglectful father.

Mothers also play a crucial role in the emotional well-being of their children. They can provide emotional support and guidance, as well as facilitate communication and reconciliation between children and fathers. It is essential for mothers to prioritize the emotional needs of their children and to avoid using their children as pawns in their own conflicts with their fathers. Mothers can also seek out support from family and friends, join support groups, and advocate for policies that support single-parent families.

Policy changes can also play a critical role in addressing the issue of absent and neglectful fathers. Policies that promote economic stability and equal access to opportunities can help reduce the stress and anxiety that can contribute to worrisome treatment and conflict in the home. Policies that promote access to affordable housing, quality healthcare, and stable employment can help reduce the financial strain on families and provide support for single parents.

Like a gardener nurturing a garden, policies that promote parental involvement and fatherhood can help to cultivate healthy and thriving families. These policies are like sunlight and water, providing the essential nutrients needed to support growth and development. They include programs that provide education and support for fathers, like fertilizers that help them to flourish. They also include policies that encourage employers to provide flexible work schedules and parental leave for fathers, like a trellis that supports healthy growth. And like a gardener who tends to the soil, policies that support co-parenting and mediation can facilitate communication and reconciliation between parents, like tending to the roots to keep the plant healthy. One policy proposal is like planting a seed, a controversial but hopeful one, offering 2x or 3x benefits for black families that practice the nuclear family. The purpose is to see if more families would reconcile, like a stimulus that encourages growth. This pilot program would benefit the whole family, offering incentives for both men and women to stay in the relationship and create a strong and stable foundation for their children to grow.

The issue of absent or neglectful fathers in the black commune is like a knot that is tightly wound, affecting children and families at the deepest levels. It is a knot that has been tied by years of systemic and societal factors, each one contributing to the tangle. Like a knot, it is not easy to unravel, requiring patience and skill to loosen the ties that bind. But with each strand that is loosened, the knot becomes a little more manageable, until we can finally see the way forward. We must approach this knot with a delicate touch, untangling each strand with care and consideration. We must look beyond the surface, to the roots of the knot, to truly understand and address the problem. Only then can we begin to create a more equitable and just society for all. Former President Barack Obama highlighted the need for fathers to take responsibility for their children, emphasizing the importance of actively participating in their lives. However, societal barriers such as poverty, racism, and dismal profiles contribute to the alienation and neglect of black fathers, making it difficult to break free from the cycle of neglect and marginalization.

Other prominent black Americans, such as Will Smith and Queen Latifah, have also emphasized the importance of fatherhood in their own lives. Will Smith believes in being a man of his word and taking care of his responsibilities, while Queen Latifah acknowledges the role of fathers in providing emotional support and guidance to their children.

The absence of a father in a child's life is like a deep wound that can fester and grow over time. It can leave a lasting scar on the child's emotional well-being, like a mark that never quite fades away. But like a skilled surgeon, we can repair the wound and promote healing through therapy, support groups, and positive male examples. We can help the child to build a strong sense of self-worth and identity, like a sturdy scaffold that supports growth and development. And like a gardener cultivating a garden, we can help the child to discover their own interests and goals, like planting a seed that will grow into a beautiful and unique flower. With time and care, the wound can heal, and the child can flourish, even in the absence of their father.

Mothers are like the anchor that keeps the boat steady in choppy waters. They offer a comforting embrace and a listening ear, providing emotional support to their children when they need it most. By offering guidance and fostering communication with fathers, mothers help create a safe and stable environment that promotes emotional well-being and healing.

However, just like a tightrope walker, mothers must maintain their balance and focus to be effective. They must put their children's emotional needs first and avoid dragging them into any conflicts with fathers. This way, they can protect their children from the waves of emotional turmoil and keep them safe and secure.

As the primary caretakers, mothers carry a heavy load, juggling multiple responsibilities on a daily basis. They are like the engine that powers the family, and just like any engine, it needs regular maintenance to run smoothly. That's why mothers must prioritize their own mental health and well-being, taking care of themselves so they can take care of others.

In the end, mothers are the heart and soul of the family. They provide the foundation on which their children can build their lives. Mothers are the architects of raising outstanding citizens in society. By offering emotional support, guidance, and fostering communication with fathers, they lay the foundation for a home filled with love, safety, and warmth, which creates an environment that helps children flourish and become exceptional members of society. Through emotional support, guidance, and fostering communication with fathers, they create a nurturing environment that cultivates love, security, and warmth in the home. This foundation enables children to thrive and develop the skills and qualities needed to make a positive impact on society.

Society is like a vast and complex ecosystem, with each member playing a vital role in its functioning. Just as a single plant can wither and die without the necessary nutrients and care, a child can suffer without the love and support of their father. Like a tree that provides roots and shelter, a father gives his child a sense of home and stability. And like a bird that spreads its wings and takes flight, a father gives his child the ability to explore and grow, to reach for the stars and achieve dreams. As a society, we must recognize the importance of fathers in this delicate ecosystem and work to create a more just and equitable system that supports all parents in their efforts to raise happy and healthy children. Let us give all children the roots and wings they need to thrive and soar in life, like a garden in full bloom and a sky full of soaring birds.

CHAPTER SIX

The Role of Society and the Legal System

In this chapter, we will explore how cultural biases and pessimistic assumptions about black fathers contribute to the false belief that they are absent or uninvolved in their children's lives. We will analyze the role of the legal system in maintaining the cycle of trauma and neglect and discuss potential reforms within the legal system and societal attitudes towards black fathers and their role in their children's lives. We will also provide resources and strategies for black fathers navigating the legal system and seeking to be more involved in their children's lives.

Societal biases and systemic injustices towards black fathers contribute to the problem of absent or neglectful fathers. Research shows that these biases and injustices can have severe consequences for the well-being of their children. Children of absent or neglectful fathers are more likely to experience poor educational outcomes, higher rates of delinquency and substance abuse, and increased risk of mental health issues.

Like a plant that needs sunlight and water to grow, black fathers need positive representation in the media and popular culture to flourish and thrive in their role as caregivers. Without this essential nourishment, black fathers may feel isolated and stigmatized, as if they are living in a desert devoid of life and hope. This can lead to decreased involvement in their children's lives, like a plant that withers and dies without the proper care. And just as a plant can be affected by external factors such as climate change and pollution, black fathers can be impacted by discrimination and systemic partiality, which can create a toxic environment for father-child relationships. We must work to create a fertile ground for black fathers to thrive, with positive representation and supportive policies that encourage and empower them to be present and engaged in their children's lives. Only then can we cultivate a garden of strong and healthy families, with black fathers playing a vital and celebrated role in their children's growth and maturation.

The legal system can also contribute to the problem of absent or neglectful black fathers. Custody battles can be biased against black fathers, with courts often assuming that the mother is the better caregiver. This bias can be based on the assumption that black fathers are more predisposed to be absent or neglectful, perpetuating the detrimental assumptions.

The burden of child support payments can feel like a heavy weight on the shoulders of black fathers, weighing them down and making it difficult to move forward. The financial strain can be overwhelming, like trying to carry a boulder up a steep hill. Some fathers may feel like they have no choice but to abandon their responsibilities and enter into the welfare system just to survive. The added stress can make it challenging for fathers to remain involved in their children's lives and fight for their rights as parents.

There have been some successful efforts to address these issues. For example, the Fatherhood Research and Practice Network (FRPN) is one organization that has successfully worked to address the challenges faced by black fathers in the legal system. This national organization has created resources and programs to provide legal representation and support services that cater to the unique obstacles faced by black fathers. Another program, "My Brother's Keeper," was launched by the Obama administration to address the opportunity gap faced by young men of color. This program aims to promote responsible fatherhood and increase father involvement in the lives of their children.

Absent and neglectful black fathers is a complex issue that is heightened by discrimination within society and systemic injustices. To combat this problem, the legal system needs to be reformed, and resources and support must be provided for black fathers. Without reform, fathers will continue to face significant obstacles in custody battles and navigating the legal system. This lack of support can be devastating for fathers who want to be involved in their children's lives but are unable to do so due to systemic blockades.

Black fathers in New York and throughout the country often face significant challenges when navigating the legal system. They may not have access to the resources, they need to hire a lawyer or fight for custody, putting them at a disadvantage. This can lead to feelings of hopelessness and despair, making it difficult for them to remain involved in their children's lives. Additionally, many black fathers may be incarcerated due to economic inequality and systemic issues. Moreover, some black fathers feel that the government helped to push them out of the home as the mothers no longer tolerate them. This can have a devastating impact on their relationships with their children and contribute to the cycle of absent or neglectful fathers.

Reforms and Strategies:

There is a need for reforms within the legal system to address the biases and injustices that black fathers face. The legal system needs to take into account the individual circumstances of each case and rely less on labels and favoritism. Legal representation should be made more accessible to black fathers, and support services should be provided to help them steer the legal system.

Several states have implemented programs aimed at promoting responsible fatherhood and increasing father involvement. But more programs are needed. In California, the Child Support Services Department has launched a program called the California Parenting Institute, which provides parenting education, job training, and legal support for fathers. The program aims to help fathers regulate the legal system and become more involved in their children's lives.

Similarly, the state of Georgia has established the Fatherhood Program, which provides parenting education, job training, and legal support for fathers. The program also provides counseling and support services to help fathers build positive relationships with their children.

In New York, the Fatherhood Initiative was established to promote responsible fatherhood and increase father involvement. The program provides resources and support services to help fathers navigate the legal system, including legal representation and counseling.

One notable example is the "Daddy University" program launched in Philadelphia, which offers a range of support services to help fathers become more involved in their children's lives. The program provides job training, legal support, and parenting education to help fathers manage the legal system and build positive relationships with their children.

These programs and initiatives have shown promising results in promoting responsible fatherhood and increasing father involvement. For example, a study of the California Parenting Institute found that fathers who participated in the program were more liable to be involved in their children's lives and had better relationships with their children.

In conclusion, it is essential to show more compassion for black fathers and acknowledge the challenges they face in being involved in their children's lives. The legal system and societal attitudes need to be reformed to provide fathers with the same level of support and resources that are available to mothers. Just like mothers receive much-needed help, fathers should be accommodated and supported in their efforts to be involved in their children's lives.

Just as a tree needs strong roots to grow and thrive, children need the support and guidance of both parents to reach their full potential. A father's presence and involvement in a child's life can provide essential emotional and financial support that helps them grow and flourish. By nurturing and fortifying these roots through policies and programs that support responsible fatherhood, we can create a society that values and cherishes the contributions of all parents. A society where all children have the opportunity to grow and thrive, just like a strong and healthy tree.

As the world becomes increasingly connected through social media and technology, it is crucial that we challenge and dismantle the harmful patterns and biases that contribute to the problem of absent or neglectful black fathers. We must strive to promote leaders and create a more supportive and inclusive society that values the contributions of all parents. Together, we can weave a tapestry of acceptance and support for all families, providing children with the strong foundation they need to grow and flourish.

Successful Programs and Initiatives:

The issue of absent or neglectful black fathers contains many layers and is challenging to address. Societal biases and systemic injustices fuel this problem, which is further exacerbated by the legal system. However, there are promising programs and initiatives that aim to support black fathers and improve outcomes for their children.

Societal biases and systemic injustices play a significant role in perpetuating the derogatory perception of black fathers as absent or neglectful. The media and popular culture often portray black fathers as being absentee or uninvolved, despite research showing that black fathers are just as likely to be involved in their children's lives as fathers of other races. These adverse profiling can lead to discrimination against black fathers in the workplace and the legal system, and can have a harmful impact on their self-esteem and their children's well-being.

Regardless of these challenges, there are successful programs and initiatives aimed at supporting black fathers and improving outcomes for their children. These programs include fatherhood initiatives that provide support and resources to help black fathers remain devoted to their children's upbringing, as well as mentorship programs that connect black fathers with inspirational figures and resources to help them control the legal system.

As we seek to promote responsible fatherhood and increase father involvement, we can find hope and inspiration in the success stories of programs and initiatives across the nation. Like bright stars shining in the night sky, these programs illuminate the path towards a brighter future for black fathers and their children. Let us explore just a few of these shining stars, each one a symbol of hope and progress in the journey towards stronger families and communities.

California Parenting Institute:

The California Parenting Institute is a remarkable program that offers a range of support services to fathers, including parenting education, job training, and legal assistance. Fathers who participate in the program receive guidance on navigating the legal system and increasing their involvement in their children's lives. The program aims to break down the barriers that prevent fathers from being engaged parents and provide them with the resources they need to become positive role models for their children.

The program has been highly effective in achieving its goals. A study of the program found that fathers who participated were more inclined to be involved in their children's lives, attend parent-teacher conferences, and have better relationships with their children. The program's parenting education and job training components have also been successful in helping fathers become better providers for their families.

The California Parenting Institute is a shining example of how targeted support programs can make a significant impact on the lives of fathers and their children. By furnishing fathers with the resources they need to be engaged parents and positive role models, the program is helping to build stronger families and communities.

The Fatherhood Program Georgia:

The Fatherhood Program in Georgia is a comprehensive program designed to assist fathers in overcoming the unique challenges they face in being involved in their children's lives. The program includes parenting education, job training, and legal support to help fathers navigate the legal system and become more attentive to their children's needs.

In addition to these resources, the program also offers counseling and support services to help fathers build positive relationships with their children. Through one-on-one counseling and group therapy sessions, fathers can develop skills and techniques to improve communication and address any issues or challenges they may face in their relationships with their children.

A recent study conducted on the program found that fathers who participated had higher levels of involvement with their children than those who did not participate. This indicates that the program is effective in promoting father-child relationships and increasing father involvement.

Overall, the Fatherhood Program in Georgia serves as a valuable resource for fathers who may face unique obstacles in being present and present for their children. Via provision of comprehensive support and resources, the program helps fathers overcome these challenges and build positive, meaningful relationships with their children.

The Fatherhood Initiative New York:

The Fatherhood Initiative in New York is a comprehensive program that aims to promote responsible fatherhood and increase father involvement in their children's lives. The program offers a wide range of resources and support services to help fathers manage the legal system, including access to legal representation and counseling. Additionally, the program provides job training and other resources to help fathers become more self-sufficient, allowing them to better provide for their children.

The Fatherhood Initiative recognizes that fathers play an important role in their children's lives and offers various programs and resources to help them become more involved. The program offers parenting classes and counseling services to help fathers build positive relationships with their children and learn effective parenting skills. Additionally, the program provides job training and assistance with finding employment, helping fathers become more financially stable and able to provide for their children.

Through its various resources and support services, the Fatherhood Initiative in New York aims to break down barriers that prevent fathers from being involved in their children's lives. Studies have shown that fathers who participate in the program have higher levels of involvement with their children, leading to positive outcomes for both fathers and their children. With the provision of resources and support services to fathers, the program helps create a more compassionate and supportive society that values the contributions of all parents.

The Daddy University Program Philadelphia:

The Daddy University program in Philadelphia is a comprehensive program designed to assist fathers in becoming more involved in the lives of their children. The program has a range of support services to help fathers cope with the challenges that come with being a parent. These services include job training, legal support, and parenting education.

The legal support services provided by the program aim to help fathers handle the complexities of the legal system, including child support and custody battles. The program also offers job training to help fathers become more self-sufficient, which can lead to greater financial stability and the ability to provide more for their children.

Parenting education is another key component of the program. Fathers learn valuable skills, such as communication, conflict resolution, and child evolution, which can help them build positive relationships with their children. The program also provides counseling services to help fathers deal with the emotional challenges that come with being a parent, including stress, anxiety, and depression.

A study of the Daddy University program found that fathers who participated in the program were more likely to be involved in their children's lives and had better relationships with their children. The program has been successful in promoting responsible fatherhood and increasing father involvement, helping to build stronger families and more supportive communities.

Texas Fathers for Equal Rights Organization:

The Texas Fathers for Equal Rights organization is a valuable resource for fathers who are struggling to maintain a meaningful relationship with their children. The organization provides legal representation and support services to fathers who are fighting for custody of their children, offering them the opportunity to access quality legal representation and negotiate the often complex and confusing legal system.

In addition to legal representation, the organization also provides resources and support services to help fathers remain involved in their children's lives after a divorce or separation. This can include counseling and mediation services to help fathers and mothers establish co-parenting agreements that are in the best interests of their children. The organization also offers job training and other resources to help fathers become more self-supporting and better able to provide for their children.

Through the supply of these resources and services, the Texas Fathers for Equal Rights organization helps fathers build positive relationships with their children and play a meaningful role in their lives. The organization's efforts to promote responsible fatherhood and increase father involvement can have a noteworthy consequence on the well-being of fathers and their children, leading to stronger and more resilient families.

The programs and initiatives aimed at supporting black fathers can be seen as rays of sunlight, breaking through the clouds of discrimination and bias that have long hindered their involvement in their children's lives. With the provision of resources and support services, these rays of hope can grow into beams of light, illuminating the path towards positive outcomes for both fathers and their children. These successful programs and initiatives offer a glimmer of hope for a future where black fathers are recognized as the shining stars, making valuable contributions to their children's lives and the world around them.

CHAPTER SEVEN

Fathers: The Backbone of a Child's Life

T he role of fathers and father figures is critical in promoting the healthy development of children. The presence of a father in a child's life can have a momentous result on their well-being, while the absence of a father figure can be detrimental to their growth. Research has shown that positive paternal relationships can have a multitude of benefits for children, such as better cognitive abilities, higher academic achievement, and improved social skills. Furthermore, positive paternal relationships have been linked to lower rates of depression, anxiety, and behavioral problems in children. Fathers also contribute significantly to the enhancement of a child's sense of self-worth and identity, emphasizing their importance in a child's life.

There are numerous programs and initiatives aimed at promoting positive paternal relationships and increasing father involvement in children's lives. For example, the National Responsible Fatherhood Clearinghouse provides resources and information for fathers on topics such as child development, co-parenting, and legal issues related to fatherhood. The National Fatherhood Initiative provides training and resources for fathers and organizations working to promote positive paternal relationships, focusing on topics such as responsible fatherhood, co-parenting, and supporting fathers in their role as parents. There are also initiatives aimed at supporting fathers in specific communities, such as the Strong Fathers, Strong Families program in Detroit, which provides support and resources for black fathers in the city.

For black fathers seeking to improve their relationships with their children and be more engaged in their lives, there are a variety of means and resources available. These include seeking out support groups and resources for fathers, focusing on building positive communication with their children, and seeking to understand and address any obstacles to involvement they may face. Black fathers can also benefit from learning about the uncommon hurdles they may face as fathers in their association, examples are prejudices and adverse generalizations against black fathers.

The promotion of positive paternal relationships and the dismantling of detrimental predispositions and stereotypes towards black fathers is crucially dependent on societal influence. Addressing systemic issues such as the criminal justice system and child welfare system, which can disproportionately impact black fathers and their families, is crucial. Additionally, promoting positive paternal relationships requires a shift in societal attitudes towards fatherhood and the importance of fathers in children's lives. Challenging unfavorable misconceptions and assumptions towards black fathers and promoting positive media representations of black fatherhood are important steps.

Personal stories from black fathers and their children provide powerful examples of the positive impact of positive paternal relationships. These stories can highlight the challenges black fathers face in their role as parents, as well as the rewards and benefits of being an involved and supportive father. For example, NBA player LeBron James has stated, "Being a father is the most important role I have. It's my job to be a role model, to be there for my kids, and to help them grow and develop into the best versions of themselves." These quotes highlight the significance of positive paternal relationships and the role that father can play in promoting positive fatherhood.

Other fathers have also spoken out about the importance of fatherhood and their role as a positive influence in their children's lives. Former NFL player Tony Dungy has said, "Being a dad is the most important job I have. My children are my legacy, and I want to leave them with a legacy of love and support." Professional basketball player Dwyane Wade has also been vocal about his commitment to being a present and involved father, stating, "My kids are my life. I want to make sure that they know they can always count on me, no matter what."

These athletes serve as exemplary individuals for fathers and encourage other fathers to prioritize their role as a parent. Additionally, many father athletes have used their platform to promote positive paternal relationships and advocate for resources and support for fathers. For example, former NBA player Etan Thomas has been an active advocate for responsible fatherhood and has written books on the topic, including "Fatherhood: Rising to the Ultimate Challenge."

Positive paternal relationships are crucial to the building and well-being of children, and it is important to promote and support father involvement in their children's lives. Fortunately, there are successful programs and initiatives aimed at promoting positive paternal relationships, as well as strategies for black fathers seeking to improve their relationships with their children.

Moreover, there is a growing number of upcoming fathers who are making a difference and starting to change the image of black fathers in society. These fathers are breaking down challenges and preferences towards black fathers, and serving as role models for other fathers seeking to be more involved in their children's lives.

With the use of cell phones and social media platforms like Instagram, Facebook, and TikTok, fathers can now directly contact their children and maintain meaningful relationships with them. No longer they must go through the mother and hope to catch a glimpse of their child's life. The era of calling the house number and waiting for the mother's permission to speak with the child is long gone. In today's world, it is easier than ever for fathers to reach out and connect with their children.

Nurturing positive paternal relationships and supporting fathers in their role as parents is crucial for society. This way, we can ensure that children receive the love, support, and guidance required to ensure their maximum growth and actualization of their capabilities. As children are the future, it is critical that we take all measures possible to uplift and support them.

CHAPTER EIGHT

Moving Forward: Breaking the Cycle of Trauma and Neglect

I n a world where sensational news takes the spotlight, it's important to shed light on the often overlooked and underappreciated topic of black fatherhood. The role of black fathers in shaping the future of our children and our society cannot be understated. It is imperative that we recognize and celebrate the valuable contributions of black fathers, and work towards creating a more equitable and just society that supports them in their role as caregivers and mentors. Our children truly are the seeds that will grow into the garden of our future.

The issue of black fatherhood is a complex web that requires a delicate approach. We cannot just pluck one thread and expect the whole tapestry to unravel. Instead, we must take a comprehensive view and acknowledge the systemic and cultural factors that hold the issue in place. One of the largest contributors to this tapestry is the disproportionate representation of black fathers in the criminal justice system, pulling on multiple threads that affect the entire fabric.

According to the National Fatherhood Initiative's report, black fathers are more liable to be incarcerated than fathers of other races or ethnicities. This leads to detrimental effects on families, including financial stress, emotional distress, and a feeling of hopelessness.

Despite these challenges, there are examples of black fathers who have overcome these obstacles and become good examples for their children. One such example is Shaka Senghor, a formerly incarcerated black father who now works to promote positive paternal relationships and support fathers who are re-entering society. Senghor emphasizes the importance of forgiveness and healing for both fathers and children, stating, "We have to heal the trauma that we've experienced so that we can break the cycle of neglect and trauma in our families."

Another example is the work of the organization Fathers and Families Center in Indianapolis, which provides support and resources for fathers who are working to overcome the challenges of poverty, incarceration, and other barriers to positive paternal relationships. The organization offers programs focused on parenting skills, job training, and mental health support, all of which can help fathers become more engaged and involved in their children's lives.

In addition to these examples, there are a variety of strategies and resources available to support black fathers and promote positive paternal relationships. These include mentorship programs, fatherhood initiatives, and legal resources to help fathers with custody battles and child support issues. Additionally, technological advances have made it easier for fathers to stay connected with their children, even if they are not living in the same household. Social media platforms such as Instagram, Facebook, and

TikTok can provide opportunities for fathers to communicate with their children and build positive relationships.

Just like an iceberg, the issue of absent or neglectful black fathers has hidden depths that cannot be overlooked. While some may see them as mere "deadbeat" parents or "sperm donors," the truth is that there are systemic and cultural factors at play that contribute to the problem. In order to truly address this issue, we must promote positive paternal relationships and provide the necessary support and resources for fathers to break the cycle of trauma and neglect. Accordingly, we can uncover the hidden depths and create a brighter future for black fathers and their children.

The cycle of trauma and neglect in black fatherhood is a deep-rooted issue that is not easily broken. It is like a dark cloud that hangs over the lives of black fathers, casting a shadow on their ability to be present and involved in their children's lives. This cycle is frequently continued by societal prejudices and derogatory generalizations that depict black fathers as missing and disinterested in their children's lives.

The systemic inequality against black fathers are deeply ingrained and can be seen in the media, where they are often portrayed as drug dealers, criminals, and absent fathers. These unfavorable characterizations not only harm black fathers' reputation but also make it harder for them to find employment and housing. The irony of this situation is that the more society perceives black fathers as uninvolved and absent, the more they are pushed away from their children, perpetuating the cycle of trauma and neglect.

Substance abuse is another major challenge that black fathers face when trying to break this cycle. Addiction is like a heavy chain that keeps them tied down and unable to be present in their children's lives. Addiction can lead to neglect, absenteeism, and strained relationships with their children.

The imagery of addiction is like a raging storm that destroys everything in its path, leaving behind a trail of destruction and broken relationships.

A study conducted by the Substance Abuse and Mental Health Services Administration found that children of fathers with substance use disorders were more likely to experience emotional and behavioral problems. This is a foreshadowing of the long-term effects of substance abuse on children and the disappointing impact it can have on their lives.

Notwithstanding these challenges, there is hope for black fathers who struggle with addiction. The Fathers for a Lifetime program in New York City is a metaphorical lifeboat that provides support and resources for fathers in recovery. This program offers a lifeline to fathers who are struggling with addiction by providing them with counseling, parenting classes, and support groups.

The cycle of trauma and neglect in black fatherhood is a complex issue that requires both systemic change and individual support for black fathers. While initiatives such as the Fathers for a Lifetime program provide crucial resources for fathers struggling with addiction, society often holds pessimistic attitudes and structural inequities towards black fathers, which can contribute to the belief that they are less involved or absent in their children's lives. This can create a cycle that is difficult to break, as these beliefs can become ingrained in individuals and society as a whole.

The media plays a crucial role in shaping these harmful myths and cultural prejudices, sustaining the image of black fathers as absent and uninvolved in their children's lives. To break the cycle of trauma and neglect, there needs to be a shift in the story, with more positive images of black fathers in the media. Shows like "The Cosby Show" and "Sanford and Son" showcased positive and prominent black fathers, offering a counter-narrative to the harmful and unfounded assumptions that have unfairly burdened black fathers for an extensive period.

Ultimately, black fathers have an image problem not only in America but in the world. In order to help improve the public image of black fathers, it is significant for the media to include more positive representations and highlight outstanding black fathers as role models. This will not only break the cycle of trauma and neglect but also provide the necessary support for black fathers to be active and involved parents. In addition, black fathers need to step up in a big way!

Providing Resources and Support for Children:

As we look towards breaking the cycle of neglect and trauma in black fatherhood, it is key to remember that children are not just silent observers in this process. They too are active participants who require resources and support to help them amidst the emotional pain that often comes with neglect and trauma.

One of the most powerful symbols of this reality is the broken heart. Children who experience neglect and trauma often feel like their hearts have been shattered into a million pieces. Providing resources and support is like offering them a way to mend those pieces back together, to restore their heart and make them whole again.

Metaphorically speaking, providing resources and support for children is like giving them a lifeboat to sail the rough waters of neglect and trauma. Without this support, they may feel like they are drowning, struggling to keep their head above water as the waves of emotional pain continue to crash down on them.

Ironically, while the focus of breaking the cycle of neglect and trauma in black fatherhood is on fathers, the most important beneficiaries are often the children. Foreshadowing what could happen if we ignore their needs, studies have shown that children who experience neglect and trauma are more likely to have emotional and behavioral problems, which can lead to poor academic performance, substance abuse, and even criminal behavior later in life.

To a kid, neglect and trauma can feel like a monster that is constantly lurking in the shadows, waiting to pounce on vulnerable children. But providing resources and support is like shining a light in the darkness, exposing the monster and empowering children to confront and overcome it.

Some children equate neglect and trauma can be like a mountain that seems impossible to climb. But with the right resources and support, children can become like mountain climbers, scaling those peaks one step at a time until they reach the summit of healing and wholeness.

Also, according to some children, the sound of neglect and trauma can be like a drumbeat that never stops, pounding in the ears of vulnerable children. But with resources and support, they can learn to dance to a different beat, one that is filled with hope, healing, and joy.

Moreover, we can envision children who are struggling with the pain of neglect and trauma as wounded birds who cannot fly. But with the right resources and support, they can become like eagles, soaring to new heights and reaching their full potential.

In order to end the cycle of neglect and trauma in black fatherhood, it is critical to prioritize providing resources and support for children. One way to support children is through counseling services, which can provide them with a safe space to discuss their emotions and experiences. Counseling can help children to develop coping mechanisms and resourcefulness, which are essential for long-term recovery.

Mentoring programs can also be helpful for children who have experienced neglect and trauma. These programs offer a positive influence and can provide a sense of belonging for children who may feel isolated or disconnected from others.

Children need avenues to express their feelings and emotions in a constructive way, especially when coping with the trauma of absent or neglectful fathers. Along with counseling and mentorship, art, music, or sports can serve as channels for children to channel their energy and emotions into something positive. These creative outlets can be a symbol of hope, providing children with a way to move forward with their pain and connect with others who share similar experiences.

Co-parenting and communication are essential to breaking the cycle of neglect and trauma in black fatherhood. Encouraging healthy communication between parents and promoting an active role for both parents in the lives of their children can help to create a supportive and nurturing environment for them.

Moreover, it is unfortunate that most children do not have a healthy outlet to express their pain and frustration, unlike the football player who is able to channel his emotions through aggressive training. Without such outlets, children may resort to destructive behavior like abusing their siblings, kicking holes in the wall, or even exhibiting bullying tendencies. As they grow older and stronger, this deep-seated anger and resentment can lead to violent behavior, causing harm to themselves and others.

It is crucial to provide children with a safe and constructive way to deal with their emotions. Sports can be a great avenue for this, but not all children are interested or have access to such opportunities. Therefore, it is important to explore other options, such as counseling services or creative outlets like music or art, to help children process and express their pain in a healthy way.

By acknowledging the emotional needs of children and providing them with appropriate resources and support, we can help prevent the formation of destructive behaviors and promote positive mental health. Let us strive to create a safe and nurturing environment for children, where they can feel heard, understood, and empowered to cope with the challenges of life.

Encouraging Father Accountability:

Breaking the cycle of neglect and trauma in black fatherhood requires a diverse approach that involves a combination of strategies and solutions. One such strategy is encouraging father accountability. This approach is all about holding fathers responsible for their actions while providing them with the support and resources they need to be successful parents.

The weight of unfair societal expectations can be crushing for black fathers, who are often held to an unattainable standard. This creates a cycle of negativity and resentment, making it difficult for black fathers to be successful parents. It's like they are carrying a heavy burden on their shoulders, one that they didn't choose but were assigned by society. This burden can cause many to feel defeated, hopeless, and angry, further reinforcing the harmful assumptions and prejudices about black fathers. It's time to lift this burden and allow black fathers to be judged on their individual merits, rather than held back by societal prejudices.

To address this issue, it is necessary to examine the cultural and societal factors that sustain these awful generalizations and stereotypes. For example, the media often portrays black fathers as absentee or uninvolved, perpetuating the cycle of neglect and trauma. This is a metaphorical chain that weighs black fathers down, making it harder for them to be present in their children's lives.

Addressing these cultural and societal factors is crucial to breaking the cycle of neglect and trauma in black fatherhood. It involves challenging harmful stereotypes and dismal connotations, creating more positive images of black fatherhood, and providing black fathers with the resources and support they need to be successful parents. For example, initiatives like the National Responsible Fatherhood Clearinghouse offer resources and support to fathers, helping them to become more involved in their children's lives.

Encouraging father culpability is an important part of this process. It involves holding fathers responsible for their actions, including financial support, emotional support, and physical presence. This is a foreshadowing of the long-term benefits of father reckoning, including improved outcomes for children, better mental health for fathers, and stronger family relationships.

Lastly, encouraging father responsibility is an important step in breaking the cycle of neglect and trauma in black fatherhood. However, it is worth saying that this is not an easy road. Fathers should not be easily persuaded to give up on their children and ignore "baby mama drama." They must be prepared for an uphill battle and must tackle the problem head-on if they want to have a lasting relationship with their offspring.

The journey of fatherhood is like climbing a steep mountain. It is difficult, but the reward at the top is worth the struggle. Building a relationship with a child who does not live with you and may be susceptible to negative stories about you is a challenging task. The journey is like walking through a storm, but once you emerge on the other side, the sun shines bright. It takes a lot of effort, commitment, and obligation to build a lasting relationship with your child.

Fathers must be accountable for their actions and must take responsibility for their role as a parent. This is a metaphorical key that unlocks the door to a positive and meaningful relationship with their children. It involves being present, providing emotional and financial support, and working through any challenges that may arise. Giving up is not an option!

Building ownership among black fathers is an essential measure in ending the vicious cycle of neglect and trauma in black fatherhood. It demands that fathers acknowledge their actions, give emotional and financial support, and stay present in their children's lives. The path of fatherhood is akin to walking on a tightrope, where a father must maintain a delicate balance and focus to move ahead and establish a robust relationship with their children, even if the mother is not supportive.

Black fathers face many obstacles, like not having enough money, unfair treatment because of their skin color, and not having enough resources to help them. It's like they're sailing a ship through a stormy sea. But, with help from others and hard work, they can make things better for themselves and their children.

Sometimes, fathers struggle with addiction, which makes it hard for them to be there for their kids. Addiction is like a big weight that pulls them down. But, stories of other fathers who have overcome addiction can give them hope and inspiration to do the same.

To help black fathers and their children, we need to work together to make things better for everyone. It's like being on a big team where everyone helps each other. With teamwork and support, we can all make a brighter future for ourselves and those we love.

Anthony Roberson is an example of a father who overcame addiction and broke the cycle of trauma and neglect. Roberson's journey was like climbing a mountain. He faced obstacles such as incarceration, addiction, and a broken relationship with his children. However, he never gave up on his children and worked hard to rebuild his relationship with them.

Roberson's personal story is a foreshadowing of the success that is possible when fathers take accountability for their actions and work to build positive relationships with their children. His story provides inspiration and hope to other fathers struggling with addiction, showing them that it is possible to break the cycle of trauma and neglect and build a strong relationship with their children.

In addition to personal stories of success, programs and initiatives aimed at promoting positive paternal relationships can also provide support for fathers. One such program is the National Responsible Fatherhood Clearinghouse, which offers resources and support to fathers looking to build a stronger relationship with their children.

The journey of fatherhood is not without its obstacles, but it is essential to remember that everything worthwhile is difficult. Building a strong relationship with your child requires dedication, perseverance, and a willingness to tackle challenges head-on. It is like a marathon, not a sprint. It takes time, effort, and commitment to cross the finish line.

Importance of education, raising awareness, and advocating for positive paternal relationships

Education is the key that unlocks the door to better decision-making, which leads to brighter outcomes. One of the most critical steps in promoting positive paternal relationships and improving outcomes for black fathers and their children is education and awareness. Education is like a ray of light that shines a spotlight on the specialized impediments faced by black fathers and the harmful effects of discouraging generalizations and cultural prejudices. Awareness is like a beacon that guides us towards a more just and equitable society.

There are numerous examples of how education and awareness can help promote positive paternal relationships. For instance, organizations like Fathers & Families Center in Indiana provide support for fathers who are trying to establish or maintain relationships with their children from a distance. This type of organization offers counseling, education, and resources to help fathers identify the challenges of long-distance parenting. This is like a life raft that helps fathers stay afloat in the choppy waters of long-distance parenting.

Additionally, education and awareness can help to dispel myths and mislabels about black fathers who live out of state. These fathers often face unfair assumptions about their involvement in their children's lives, leading to discrimination in the workplace and legal system. Advocating for policies that support long-distance parenting and recognizing the importance of maintaining positive relationships with non-custodial parents can help to break down these obstacles.

Another critical issue that education and awareness can help to address is drug addiction and its impact on black fatherhood. Substance abuse is like a dark cloud that hangs over fathers and their children, leading to neglect and trauma. Organizations like the National Fatherhood Initiative offer resources and support for fathers struggling with addiction, including counseling and treatment options. This is like a lighthouse that guides fathers towards a path of recovery and helps them to build positive relationships with their children.

I will strongly state that the image of black fathers ultimately resides with black fathers themselves. Education and awareness are powerful tools that can help fathers stay the course and overcome the peculiar limitations they face. It is important to address issues such as drug addiction, which can erode someone's ability to be self-accountable and have a lasting impact on fatherhood.

However, it is crucial to acknowledge the disparities that exist within the black experience when it comes to fatherhood. Fathers who are illiterate or lack resources may face additional challenges when it comes to accessing education and support. This is like trying to navigate a maze without a map. Additionally, fathers who do not actively seek help through community initiatives may also face challenges to improving their relationships with their children.

Like climbing a mountain, overcoming the challenges that black fathers face requires a steadfast commitment to taking accountability for their actions and building positive relationships with their children. By actively seeking out education and support, fathers can break down hurdles and reach new heights, providing a brighter future for themselves and their children.

Just as a potter molds clay into a beautiful vessel, black fathers have the power to shape their own image and that of their children through their actions. By seeking education, resources, and support, they can turn their experiences into something beautiful and break the cycle of trauma and neglect. Let us all join hands and help them shape a brighter future for themselves and their children, creating a more just and equitable society for all.

Promoting positive paternal relationships: Resources and strategies.

Breaking the cycle of trauma and neglect in black fatherhood is not an easy task, but it is a necessary one. It requires a concerted effort from individuals, communities, and society as a whole. Fortunately, there are numerous resources and strategies available for those seeking to promote positive paternal relationships and break down handicaps.

One strategy is mentorship programs, which connect black fathers with guiding lights and resources for navigating the legal system and improving relationships with their children. The 100 Black Men of America organization is a prime example of this approach. The 100 Black Men of America organization is a powerful mentorship program that connects black fathers with encouraging models and resources for navigating the legal system and improving relationships with their children. With chapters in cities across the country, this organization provides mentoring, tutoring, and other support services to help fathers become better parents and community leaders.

The 100 Black Men of America program aims to provide guidance and support to young people and empower them to make positive decisions and achieve success in their lives. It also offers career development opportunities for fathers, including job training and networking opportunities, to help them become more self-sufficient and provide for their families.

Through this program, black fathers can build relationships with positive role models, gain valuable skills and knowledge, and become more active and engaged parents. By empowering black fathers to be leaders in their communities and advocates for their children, the 100 Black Men of America program is making a significant impact in breaking the cycle of trauma and neglect in black fatherhood.

Another strategy is community-based initiatives, such as the Real Dads Read program and the Fathers United program. The Real Dads Read program and the Fathers United program, both offered by Fathers Incorporated, are community-based initiatives that offer a range of resources and support services to black fathers. The Real Dads Read program focuses on promoting literacy and reading by providing books and hosting reading events for fathers and their children. The Fathers United program, on the other hand, offers mentorship opportunities and support services such as job training and legal assistance to help fathers become more involved in their children's lives.

By engaging with these initiatives, black fathers can develop the skills and knowledge they need to be effective parents and role models. These programs offer a supportive gathering that values the contributions of black fathers and empowers them to be advocates for their children.

In order to ensure a brighter future for black fathers and their children, it is essential to recognize and dismantle the systemic hurdles that contribute to derogatory assumptions and bleak predispositions. It is like clearing a path through a dense forest. By pushing for policy changes that support positive paternal relationships and address injustices within the legal system, we can create a more equitable society that values the contributions of black fathers. This includes advocating for father-friendly workplaces and flexible schedules that enable fathers to spend more time with their children, providing them with the support and resources they need to be present and engaged parents.

Education and awareness are also critical components in promoting positive paternal relationships and breaking the cycle of trauma and neglect. This includes educating the public about the importance of involved fatherhood and The effect of adverse perceptions and prejudices. It also involves providing education and resources for fathers themselves, including parenting classes and access to information about child development and co-parenting.

Promoting positive paternal relationships and breaking the cycle of trauma and neglect in black fatherhood requires a collective effort from individuals, communities, and society as a whole. While education, awareness, advocacy, and community-based initiatives are critical components in achieving this goal, it is also important to acknowledge the need for other people to step up if the father is not available.

In the journey of life, children need influential leaders to guide them, and uncles, coaches, big brothers, and stepfathers can serve as beacons of hope. They offer support, love, and guidance, just like a lighthouse that guides ships to shore safely. It takes a collective effort to raise a child, and every person who can lend a hand has a role to play. Collaboration and mutual support are key to building a society where children flourish and families prosper. When we come together and uplift each other, we create a powerful force for positive change that benefits everyone.

The benefits of positive paternal relationships are clear. Children with involved fathers are more likely to do well in school, have higher self-esteem, and have better mental health outcomes. They are also less likely to engage in risky behaviors and criminal activity.

At the heart of this issue lies a seed of hope - the power to break the chains of neglect and despair in black fatherhood. It is our collective responsibility to nourish and cultivate this seed, by promoting positive paternal relationships and empowering black fathers to be role models for success and advocates for their children. With every step forward, we draw closer to a future where every child has the love, support, and guidance they need to flourish.

CHAPTER NINE

The Role of Mothers

M others have always played an essential role in raising and nurturing children, providing a stable foundation for their growth and advancement. Mothers are like the roots of a tree, providing stability and nourishment for their children to grow strong. But when the father is absent or neglectful, the tree becomes unbalanced, with the mother bearing the weight of parenting alone. This can lead to a heavy burden on the mother's shoulders, causing mental strain and exhaustion, which can affect both her and her child's wellbeing. Therefore, prioritizing mental health is crucial to ensure that the roots remain strong and healthy, allowing the tree to grow and flourish.

It is crucial for mothers to understand the impact of their behavior and attitude on their child's relationship with their absent father. Anger and bitterness can be understandable emotions in the face of neglect, abandonment, or abuse by the father. However, it is essential for mothers to be mindful of how these emotions can detrimentally affect their child's relationship with their father.

The importance of promoting healthy co-parenting relationships and communication is of great significance. Co-parenting involves working collaboratively with the child's father, even when the relationship has ended. By focusing on the best interests of the child, mothers can help to create a positive environment that promotes healthy relationships and communication between the child and both parents.

The importance of promoting healthy co-parenting relationships and communication cannot be overstated. Co-parenting involves working collaboratively with the child's father, even when the relationship has ended. By focusing on the best interests of the child, mothers can help to create a positive environment that advances healthy relationships and communication between the child and both parents.

Personal stories and perspectives from famous black mothers provide valuable insights into the unique challenges and responsibilities of raising children without a present or supportive father. Some of the most inspiring and influential black mothers include:

1- Sybrina Fulton: The mother of Trayvon Martin, who was killed by George Zimmerman in 2012, has become a prominent advocate for social justice and racial equality. She has dedicated her life to fighting for justice for her son and other victims of police brutality, while also raising awareness about the impact of gun violence on families and communities.

2- Michelle Obama: The former first lady of the United States has been an influential role model for black mothers and women around the world. Through her memoir, Becoming, she has shared her personal experiences and challenges as a mother, wife, and public figure, inspiring others to pursue their dreams and make a positive impact in their communities.

3- Maya Angelou: The renowned author and poet, who passed away in 2014, was a powerful advocate for civil rights and social justice. Her personal story of overcoming trauma and adversity has inspired countless individuals, including mothers and children, to find strength and resilience in difficult times.

4- Taraji P. Henson: The actress and activist has been a vocal advocate for mental health awareness, particularly in the black community. As a single mother, she has faced numerous challenges in raising her son, but has always been a strong and supportive presence in his life.

Studies have shown that the presence of a positive mother figure in a child's life can have significant long-term benefits. Children with involved mothers are more likely to do well in school, have higher self-esteem, and have better mental health outcomes. However, moreover crucial for mothers to prioritize their own mental health and self-care, as the demands of single parenthood can be overwhelming and stressful.

The role of black mothers in raising children without a present or supportive father cannot be emphasized enough. These mothers often carry the weight of parenting alone, facing singular difficulties and responsibilities. They provide emotional support, nurture their children, and help them manage life's challenges. Despite the difficulties they face, black mothers have demonstrated an unwavering commitment to their children and their well-being.

It is indispensable that we celebrate and recognize the hard work and dedication of black mothers. These women are doing an incredible job under challenging circumstances, and they deserve to be acknowledged and honored for their efforts. One way to do this is by presenting awards and recognizing their contributions to their families and communities.

Black fathers must step up and take responsibility for their role in their children's lives. However, until this happens, black mothers will continue to face the burden of parenting alone. We must recognize the high degree of stress that black mothers face on a daily basis and acknowledge the meaningful outcome that fathers can have on their children's lives.

While black mothers are doing their best to raise their children, there are certain life lessons that are more pronounced when they come from a father. A father's presence and involvement can provide a unique perspective and guidance for their children, helping them to deal with the challenges of life and grow into responsible, successful adults.

There are many studies and statistics that highlight the importance of black mothers in raising successful, well-adjusted children. For example, a study conducted by the National Fatherhood Initiative found that children who grow up without a father are more likely to experience poverty, drug abuse, and other disheartening outcomes. However, the study also found that children who have strong relationships with their mothers are more likely to avoid these negative outcomes and succeed in life.

In conclusion, black mothers play a critical role in raising successful, well-adjusted children. They deserve recognition, support, and resources to help them handle the challenges of parenting alone. While black fathers must step up and take responsibility for their role in their children's lives, we must also acknowledge the important contributions of black mothers and work to promote healthy co-parenting relationships and communication. In the end, by supporting and empowering black mothers, we can help to create a better future for all of our children.

I will land this chapter with this: it's a funny thing how society can be so quick to label all fathers as "deadbeats" or "sperm donors" while simultaneously holding all mothers up on a pedestal of perfection. As a single father, I've had to learn to navigate this double standard and work twice as hard to prove that good fathers do exist. It's not fair, but it's the reality we live in, and I'm determined to challenge these biases and preconceptions.

It's a peculiar world we live in. No matter what the circumstances, mothers always seem to be given a free pass, no matter how much they've messed up. From the negligent to the downright criminal, they're still hailed as saints because "mamas can't do wrong". Yet fathers, especially black fathers, seem to be held to a different standard altogether. Even children, from boys to girls, will mercilessly pound on their fathers at any opportunity. It's as if respect for black fathers is a foreign concept that has yet to be discovered.

The Responsibilities and Challenges faced by Mothers:

The challenges and responsibilities that black mothers face in raising their children without a present or supportive father are immense. According to the U.S. Census Bureau, nearly 80% of single-parent households in the United States are headed by mothers, and black mothers are more likely to be single mothers than women of other racial and ethnic groups. This means that a significant portion of black mothers are left to bear the burden of parenting alone, facing numerous challenges and obstacles along the way.

One of the biggest challenges that black mothers face is financial strain. Single mothers are more likely to live in poverty than married couples or single fathers, and this is particularly true for black mothers. In fact, black single mothers are almost twice as likely to live in poverty as white single mothers. This financial strain can lead to a range of issues, including limited access to resources and opportunities, and a lack of stability for both the mother and child.

Raising children as a single parent can be incredibly challenging for anyone, but it can be especially difficult for black mothers who often have to maneuver the emotional and financial strain of raising children without the support of their absent or neglectful fathers. These mothers have to be emotionally strong for their children and help them deal with complex feelings of abandonment and confusion, while also providing for them financially. It is a lot to handle, and these mothers often have to take on the role of not just a caregiver, but also a therapist, counselor, and support system for their children. It truly takes a lot of strength, patience, and love to be a black single mother raising children.

Despite the obstacles, black mothers have shown incredible adaptability and strength in raising their children alone. Some of the most inspiring and influential black mothers have shared their personal stories and experiences, providing valuable insights into the peculiar restraints and responsibilities of raising children without a present or supportive father.

One such example is Ursula Burns, former CEO of Xerox Corporation, who was raised by a single mother in a New York City housing project. Burns credits her mother with instilling in her the values of hard work, determination, and self-reliance, and inspiring her to pursue her dreams and succeed in business.

Another example is Mellody Hobson, co-CEO of Ariel Investments and a prominent advocate for financial literacy and education. Hobson was raised by a single mother in Chicago and has spoken publicly about the challenges she faced in navigating a complex financial system and building financial security for herself and her family.

And then there's Cathy Hughes, founder and chairperson of Urban One, a multimedia company that includes radio, television, and online platforms. Hughes was a single mother who worked multiple jobs to support her family, eventually building a media empire that has had a considerable influence on black culture and society.

These women, and countless others like them, have shown that black mothers are capable of incredible strength and robustness, even in the face of enormous challenges. However, they also highlight the need for greater support and resources for black mothers who are raising children alone, including access to education, job training, financial assistance, and emotional support.

Mothers have always played an essential role in raising and nurturing children, providing a stable foundation for their growth and skills acquisition. But when a father is absent or neglectful, the burden of parenting often falls entirely on the mother, creating additional challenges and responsibilities. When a father is absent or neglectful, mothers often have to take on additional responsibilities and challenges in raising their children. Mothers become the sole providers for their children, responsible for financial, emotional, and physical support. They may also have to juggle work, school, or other obligations while still ensuring that their children's needs are met like feeding the children, shopping for clothes, participating in school events and so on... Additionally, mothers often deal with the emotional impact of their children's absent or neglectful fathers, helping them process their feelings and heal from any trauma or neglect they may have experienced. In these situations, it can be easy for mothers to become overwhelmed and frustrated, leading to troubling outcomes for both the mother and child.

It is crucial for mothers to understand the impact of their behavior and attitude on their child's relationship with their absent father. Anger and bitterness can be understandable emotions in the face of neglect, abandonment, or abuse by the father. However, it is essential for mothers to be mindful of how these emotions can undesirably affect their child's relationship with their father.

The importance of promoting healthy co-parenting relationships and communication is of utmost importance. Co-parenting involves working collaboratively with the child's father, even when the relationship has ended. By focusing on the best interests of the child, mothers can help to create a positive environment that fosters healthy relationships and communication between the child and both parents.

Personal stories and perspectives from successful black mothers in the business world provide valuable insights into the extraordinary test and responsibilities of raising children while also building a successful career. Some of the most inspiring and influential black mothers in business include:

Ursula Burns: The former CEO of Xerox and the first black woman to lead a Fortune 500 company, Burns has been a powerful advocate for diversity and inclusion in the corporate world. As a mother of two, she has also been a vocal supporter of work-life balance and flexible work arrangements for working parents.

Rosalind Brewer: The CEO of Walgreens Boots Alliance and the first black woman to lead a Fortune 500 company in the retail industry, Brewer has been a role model for women and minorities in business. She has also been an advocate for education and workforce development, supporting programs that help young people succeed in school and find employment opportunities.

Lisa Price: The founder and CEO of Carol's Daughter, a natural beauty products company, Price has built a successful business while also being a dedicated mother of two. She has been a vocal advocate for entrepreneurship and women's empowerment, inspiring other mothers to pursue their dreams and build successful businesses.

Janice Bryant Howroyd: The founder and CEO of ActOne Group, a global staffing and workforce management company, Howroyd has been a trailblazer in the business world. As a mother of three, she has also been a vocal advocate for work-life balance and supporting working mothers in the workforce.

Studies have shown that the presence of a positive mother figure in a child's life can have significant long-term benefits. Children with involved mothers are more likely to do well in school, have higher self-esteem, and have better mental health outcomes. That said, it is crucial for mothers to prioritize their own mental health and self-care, as the demands of single parenthood can be overwhelming and stressful.

Amidst the chaos of raising children, black mothers are the anchors that keep their families grounded. They are the unsung heroes who provide a stable foundation for their children's growth and maturity, even in the absence of a father figure. Like a lighthouse in the storm, they guide their children through the rough waters of life with their unwavering love and dedication. It is time to acknowledge and honor the sacrifices and dilemmas of black mothers, and provide them with the support and resources they need to continue shining their light for their families.

As much as black mothers are praised for their hard work and dedication to their children, black fathers must also step up to the plate and take on their responsibilities. Just like two legs are needed to walk, both parents are needed to raise a child. It is important for fathers to understand the weight of their absence or neglect on their children, and take the initiative to establish a healthy co-parenting relationship with the mother. Only then can they build a strong foundation for their children to thrive and flourish.

In the journey of parenting, both mothers and fathers have important roles to play, like two wings of a bird that help it fly higher. While black mothers are often celebrated for their unwavering love and support, the importance of involved fatherhood must not be overlooked. By recognizing the critical role that both parents play in a child's upbringing, we can create a society where children can soar to their fullest potential, like a flock of birds taking flight in perfect harmony.

The Impact of a Mother's Anger and Bitterness:

Disclaimer out of fear of retaliation: Most mothers including black mothers are wonderful parents. However, this is for the minority of mothers. It is essential for mothers to be mindful of their words and actions when it comes to discussing their child's absent or neglectful father. While it is natural to feel angry or resentful towards a father who is failing to meet his obligations, expressing this anger in front of the child can have lasting paiful effects. The need to expose the father to the child or anyone else should not be a winning strategy.

Research has shown that a mother's dismal attitude towards the father can lead to a decrease in the child's emotional well-being, increased aggression, and difficulty in forming and maintaining relationships. A study published in the Journal of Family Psychology found that children who were exposed to parental conflict, including pessimistic talk about the father, had higher levels of anxiety, depression, and behavioral problems.

In addition to the emotional impact, a mother's anger and bitterness can also have legal consequences. If a mother consistently prevents the father from seeing their child or violates custody arrangements, it can result in legal repercussions and may finally harm the child's relationship with their father.

It is vital for mothers to recognize that their words and actions have a powerful impact on their children's evolution into adulthood and well-being. Instead of focusing on the adverse aspects of the absent or neglectful father, mothers should try to promote positive co-parenting relationships and foster open communication between the child and their father. It is ok to be mad at the father as we are only human; however, not in front of the children.

One example of a mother who has promoted positive co-parenting relationships is Sherri Shepherd, the comedian and actress. Despite her divorce from her son's father, she has worked to maintain a positive relationship between her son and his father. In interviews, she has emphasized the importance of putting the child's needs first and creating a healthy co-parenting relationship.

Another example is actress Halle Berry, who has spoken about the challenges of raising her children as a single mother while still maintaining a positive relationship with their father. In an interview with People magazine, she emphasized the importance of prioritizing the child's well-being and creating a peaceful co-parenting relationship.

Mothers hold the power to shape their children's perception of their father, for better or for worse. Like a gardener tending to a fragile seedling, they must cultivate a healthy co-parenting relationship and nurture open communication. Consequently, they can shield their children from the detrimental impact of an absent or neglectful father and help them to grow into emotionally stable and resilient adults. It is an immense responsibility, but one that can yield a fruitful harvest for generations to come.

In conclusion, it should be expressed loud and clear that not all mothers speak destructively about absent or neglectful fathers. However, when it does happen, it can have a negative impact on the child's relationship with their father. Equally essential to acknowledge the high levels of stress that mothers face when they have to take on both the roles of mother and father. We are not blaming mothers, but rather, providing an alternative perspective in the hopes of starting a conversation about this topic. Mothers are incredibly important in our society and all mothers are doing their best to raise their children in difficult circumstances. It is encouraged to celebrate and recognize their hard work and contributions to the well-being of their children and communities.

Promoting Healthy Co-Parenting Relationships and Communication:

Co-parenting can be a tricky task, especially when the relationship between the parents is strained. However, with the right mindset and strategies, It has the potential to be a rewarding and satisfying experience. One way to achieve healthy co-parenting is through the use of humor. Humor can be a great tool to break down blockades and help parents see things from each other's perspectives.

Studies have shown that co-parenting can have numerous benefits for children, including improved academic performance, increased self-esteem, and better mental health. Children who have positive relationships with both parents tend to have fewer behavioral problems and are less likely to engage in risky behaviors.

One example of successful co-parenting is the relationship between actor Will Smith and his ex-wife, Sheree Zampino. Despite their divorce, they have maintained a positive co-parenting relationship and prioritize their children's needs above their own personal differences. They often post playful photos and videos on social media, showcasing their humorous and lighthearted approach to co-parenting.

Another example is the co-parenting relationship between business mogul Russell Simmons and his ex-wife, Kimora Lee Simmons. Despite their divorce, the two have remained committed to co-parenting their two daughters and have even worked together professionally on various business ventures. Their ability to put their differences aside for the sake of their children serves as a powerful example of the importance of positive co-parenting relationships in the African American community.

While co-parenting can be a challenge, it is necessary for mothers to remember that it is not their sole responsibility to make it work. Fathers must also take an active role in co-parenting and be willing to put in the effort to build a healthy relationship with their children. Mothers can encourage this by setting clear boundaries, communicating openly and honestly, and focusing on the child's needs.

In the world of co-parenting, involving extended family members can be a valuable resource for the child's growth. This is especially true for African American families, where grandparents, aunts, uncles, and other family members have historically played a vital role in child-rearing. Involving the father's side of the family can also help to maintain a sense of connection to the child's paternal heritage, even in the absence of the father. However, it is paramount for all family members to remember that this is not about taking sides or judging the parents. Instead, it is about promoting healthy communication and relationships between the parents and providing support and guidance for the child's well-being. Extended family members who work together in a positive and non-judgmental way can help to create a stable and loving environment for the child to thrive in.

Strategies for Becoming a Great Father

Becoming a great father is like a journey through a winding path with ups and downs, moments of victory, and challenges to overcome. It's a journey that requires a lot of effort and dedication, but there may not always be a big reward or recognition waiting for you at the end. It's a path that requires dedication, effort, and the willingness to learn and grow. However, with the right strategies and mindset, any father can become a positive force in the lives of their children, no matter the obstacles they face.

One key strategy for effective fatherhood is positive co-parenting. Like two sides of a coin, mothers and fathers both play critical roles in the lives of their children, and it's essential to work together to create a loving, stable environment. By communicating openly, respecting each other's opinions, and putting the needs of the child first, fathers can build a strong partnership with the mother and create a foundation of support that benefits everyone.

Another strategy is building a strong relationship with the child. Like a gardener tending to a young sapling, fathers must invest time, effort, and care into nurturing their relationship with their child. By spending quality time together, listening attentively, and modeling positive behaviors, fathers can foster a strong bond that will last a lifetime.

When it comes to discipline, fathers must strike a delicate balance. Like a captain guiding a ship through treacherous waters, fathers must set boundaries and enforce consequences when necessary. However, it's equally important to use positive discipline techniques that promote healthy development and avoid harmful or ineffective forms of discipline.

Perhaps the most important strategy for effective fatherhood is perseverance. Like a marathon runner pushing through the pain and fatigue, fathers must stay committed to their goal of being a loving, involved father, even when faced with obstacles and challenges. By staying the course, seeking support when needed, and always putting the needs of their children first, fathers can become a positive force in their lives and make a lasting impact on their future.

In conclusion, becoming a great father is a journey that requires effort, dedication, and a willingness to learn and grow. And sometimes to be a great father all it takes is for you to be present. As a father of three children with different personalities and aspirations, I know firsthand that being an effective father is not easy. However, my children mean the world to me, and I am committed to doing everything in my power to be a positive force in their lives.

As a father, I've come to learn that each child has their own unique traits and temperaments. My oldest daughter just turned 17 and tends to wait until the day of her birthday to remind me that it's her special day and if you happen to forget, then all hail breaks loose, while my 14-year-old daughter plans and plots her birthday wishes up to 6 months in advance.

Their career aspirations are just as different. My oldest daughter aspires to become a nurse, while my younger daughter wants to pursue a career in writing. My middle child, who is a boy, is currently interested in becoming a rapper or a gamer. While he has a natural talent for athletics, he is currently lacking the motivation and drive to practice religiously.

Being a father to such diverse children is not easy, but it's an experience that has taught me the importance of understanding and celebrating their individual qualities and ambitions. I am committed to supporting and guiding them as they navigate their way through life and pursue their dreams.

One lesson I've learned on this journey is that it's important not to focus on being your child's best friend. As a father, your role is to provide guidance, support, and discipline when necessary. While it may be difficult at times especially if you don't live in the same home as the child, staying true to this role is ultimately what will make you a respected and valued figure in your child's life.

At the end of the day, there is no one right way or wrong way to be a great father. What matters most is that you approach your role with love and a commitment to doing what's best for your child. As a final point, I will leave you with this, being a good dad is like building a tall tower out of blocks. You need to keep going, ask for help when you need it, and make sure you're putting the important pieces first, just like your child. When you do this, you have the foundation to create something pretty special and memorable that will be key to create positive citizens in society which will be passed down to future generations.

EPILOGUE

Reflections on Fatherhood

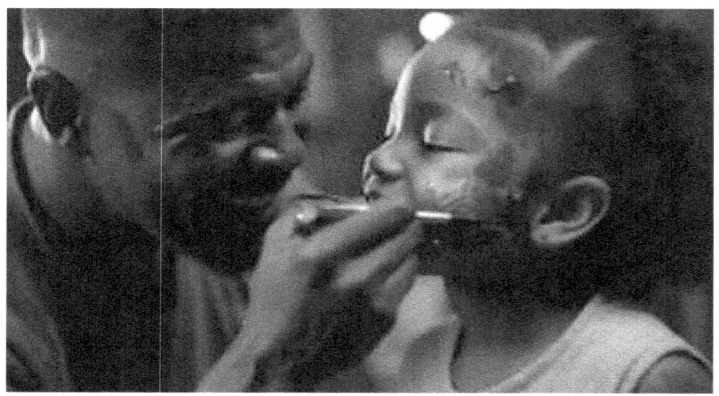

F atherhood is a winding path that is often unpredictable, with twists and turns that bring both elation and heartache. Yet, despite the bumps in the road, the journey of fatherhood is a priceless and fulfilling adventure. For black fathers, this journey is filled with unique challenges and hurdles that require an unwavering commitment and strength of character to overcome. Despite the odds, black fathers continue to strive to be positive role models and advocates for their children, proving that the journey of fatherhood is a noble and rewarding pursuit.

Throughout this book, we have explored the struggles and plights that black fathers face in America. We have also discussed the emotional impact of absentee fathers and the potential long-term effects on the psychological health of their children. However, we have also highlighted the importance of recognizing and supporting black fathers in their role as caregivers and role models.

Fatherhood is like a hidden gem that often goes unnoticed, overshadowed by the dazzling spotlight of motherhood. While Mother's Day is showered with flowers and gifts, Father's Day often goes uncelebrated, with significantly fewer cards and presents sold. However, the value of fatherhood cannot be overlooked, especially for black fathers who have faced distinct challenges throughout history. But the significance of fatherhood should not be measured by commercial standards.

Black fathers have faced significant obstacles that have prevented them from being fully present and involved in their children's lives. These limitations can range from cultural prejudices to structural inequities, which can impact their ability to provide for their children and be seen as empowering figures. Despite these obstacles, it is of utmost importance to recognize the vital role that black fathers play in their children's lives, and to provide them with the support and resources they need to be strong caregivers and role models. Fathers must take a stand and make their children a top priority, even in the face of adversity.

Studies have shown that the presence of a father in a child's life can have a considerable implication on their well-being, including higher academic achievement, lower risk of delinquency, and better behavioral health. But the absence of a father can have equally significant troubling effects, including increased risk of poverty, behavioral problems, and mental health issues.

It is imperative to acknowledge and address the challenges that black fathers face, including the disproportionate impact of systemic racism and discrimination on their ability to provide for their families. This can be done through policy changes and greater access to resources such as education, job training, healthcare, and mental health services.

Additionally, promoting positive co-parenting relationships and communication can help to strengthen the role of fathers in the lives of their children. This can involve breaking down stigmas around seeking help and support, as well as providing resources and support for both parents to work together for the benefit of their children.

As a black father who has had to deal with the family court system multiple times in order to maintain a relationship with my three children from two different mothers, I understand firsthand the uncommon hurdles and obstacles that black fathers face in our society. It has not been an easy journey, and there have been many ups and downs, but I have remained dedicated to being the best father that I can be.

Despite the difficulties and roadblocks that I have faced, I have never given up on my children or on my role as a father. For me, nothing else matters more than being a father and having a relationship with my children. Even though my relationships with their mothers may have ended, my love and commitment to my children will never falter. I do not place blame on anyone, including the mothers, for the challenges that I have faced as a father. However, I do believe that it is necessary to acknowledge the struggles that black fathers face and to urge all parents, particularly mothers, to work towards creating an environment that is conducive to positive co-parenting and to fostering strong relationships between fathers and their children.

Black fathers, and all fathers, are unsung heroes in the journey of raising children. It is key for mothers and fathers to work together and acknowledge each other's contributions in the flourishing of their children. While their roles may differ, they are equally valuable in creating a nurturing and supportive environment for the children. Like a musical harmony, the roles of fathers and mothers blend together to create a beautiful melody that resonates throughout the family. It's natural for one parent to feel like they are carrying a heavier load, but it is of great importance to appreciate and support each other for the benefit of the children.

In Chapter 1, I posed the question of whether black fathers are good or bad. As I present my evidence, I leave it to you to decide for yourself. However, as I reflect on my own experience as a father, I believe that being a great dad is something that one is born with. It's not a skill that can be taught or learned, but rather a deep desire within a man's heart to be present for his children and to be a positive influence in their lives.

This desire to be a great dad is what drives black fathers to persevere through the challenges and obstacles that they face. Despite the hurful preconceptions and prejudices that society has imposed on them, many black fathers have continued to be present and engaged in their children's lives. They understand the importance of being a positive role model and instilling values such as respect, hard work, and determination in their children.

The role of black fathers in providing for and nurturing their children cannot be understated, and it is central to recognize and celebrate their dedication and sacrifices.

Studies show that black fathers today are doing better than previous generations which is a testament to their commitment and grit in the face of systemic and cultural challenges. This progress should be acknowledged and celebrated, but there is still much work to be done to ensure that black fathers are given the support and resources they need to be fully involved in their children's lives. By dismantling harmful labels, promoting positive paternal relationships and adopting co-parenting skills, we can create a brighter future for black fathers and their families. I leave you with some great stories from prominent African American family which should make us happy as the future looks bright based on these wonderful examples of the power of fatherhood.

As we look towards the future, let us draw inspiration from the powerful examples of African American fathers who have left an indelible mark on their families and communities. These fathers have shown that with dedication, love, and commitment, anything is possible. Their stories serve as a beacon of hope, illuminating the path for the next generation of fathers who will continue to shape the world with their unwavering strength and toughness.

Exhibit A - Defense:

1- Barack Obama, former President of the United States, is a father of two daughters. He has spoken about the importance of balancing work and family, saying "My job as a husband and father, and my job as President, are one and the same - and it's something that I try to do every day." Obama has also emphasized the importance of being present for his daughters, stating "I want to make sure that I'm not just a present father, but a good father."

2- LeBron James, NBA player, is the father of three children. He has spoken about the importance of being present for his family despite his busy schedule, saying "No matter what's going on in my life or career, my family always comes first. Being a father is my top priority, and I'm grateful for the moments I get to spend with my kids."

3- Denzel Washington, actor and producer, is the father of four children. He has spoken about the role of fatherhood in his life, saying "Being a father is the most important job I've ever had. My children are my greatest accomplishment and my biggest inspiration."

4- Kevin Hart, comedian and actor, is the father of four children. He has spoken about the importance of being a present father and role model for his children, saying "I want to be a father that's actually there, not just financially but emotionally and mentally, too. It's my job to raise great human beings."

5- Will Smith, actor and musician, is the father of three children. He has spoken about the importance of being a positive role model for his children, saying "As a father, it's important to me to lead by example and show my children the importance of hard work, determination, and kindness."

6- Jamie Foxx, actor and musician, is the father of two daughters. He has spoken about his dedication to being a present father despite his busy schedule, saying "No matter what, my daughters always come first. I make sure I'm there for them and present in their lives. It's the most important thing to me."

7- Steph Curry, NBA player, is the father of three children. He has spoken about the importance of being a present and involved father, saying "Being a dad is the most important job I have. I want to make sure my kids know they are loved and supported, and that I'm there for them no matter what."

8- Dwayne "The Rock" Johnson, actor and former professional wrestler, is the father of three daughters. He has spoken openly about the importance of being a present and engaged father in his children's lives, despite his busy schedule. In an interview with Oprah Winfrey, Johnson spoke about his struggles with depression and how becoming a father helped him find purpose and meaning in life. He said, "Being a dad, being a father, is the greatest job I have ever had...It's the greatest job I will ever have."

9- Dwyane Wade, former NBA player, is the father of four children. He has been open about his journey as a father, including his struggles with co-parenting and custody battles. Wade has emphasized the importance of being present for his children, saying "For me, being a father is the most important job in the world...it's not about how much money you make or what kind of job you have, it's about being there for your kids."

10- LL Cool J, rapper and actor, is the father of four children. He has spoken about the importance of being present and supportive for his family, saying "As a father, I want to be there for my children in every way possible. Whether it's attending their games and performances or just being a listening ear, I want them to know that I'm always here for them."

11- Chance the Rapper, musician, is the father of two daughters. He has spoken about the importance of being present for his children, saying "I want my kids to know that they can always come to me and that I'm always going to be there for them. I want to be a present father and make sure they know they are loved."

12- John Legend, musician and activist, is the father of two children. He has spoken about the importance of being a present and involved father, saying "Being a dad is the most important thing I'll ever do. I want to make sure I'm there for my kids and that they know they can always count on me."

13- Bill Cosby, Comedian and actor, is the father of 5 children. He has emphasized the importance of being present and involved in his children's lives, and has stressed the role of the father as a provider and protector for his family. In an interview with Oprah Winfrey, Cosby said "I've learned that a father's responsibility is to protect and provide for his children. That's the bottom line. Protect them from harm and provide them with what they need to succeed." He also talked about the joy and fulfillment that comes from being a father, saying "There's nothing like being a father. It's the most wonderful thing in the world."

14- Pharrell Williams, musician and producer, is the father of four children. He has spoken about the joy and fulfillment of being a father, saying "Being a dad is the most rewarding thing I've ever done. I love being there for my kids and seeing them grow and learn."

15- Idris Elba, actor and musician, is the father of two children. He has spoken about the joy and fulfillment of being a father, saying "Being a dad is the best thing that's ever happened to me. I love being there for my kids and watching them grow into amazing human beings."

16- Ice Cube, rapper and actor, is the father of four children. He has spoken about the importance of being a present and involved father, saying "Being a dad is the most important job in the world. I want to make sure my kids know they are loved and supported, and that they can always count on me."

17- Common, musician and actor, is the father of one daughter. He has spoken about the impact his daughter has had on his life, saying "My daughter has taught me so much about love and patience and being present...it's the greatest gift I could ever ask for." Common has also emphasized the importance of being a positive role model for his daughter, stating "I want to show her what it means to be a strong black man, to be respectful and caring and compassionate."

18- Michael Jordan, former NBA player, is the father of five children. He has been open about the challenges of balancing his career and family life, stating "As a father, you always have to make sacrifices...it's not always easy, but it's necessary." Jordan has also emphasized the importance of being present for his children, saying "I want to be there for them as much as I can, to support them and guide them and help them become the best versions of themselves."

19- Usher, musician and actor, is the father of two sons. He has spoken about the importance of being a positive role model for his children, stating "As a father, I have to lead by example...I want my sons to see what it means to be a good man, to be respectful and honest and hardworking." Usher has also emphasized the importance of being present for his children, saying "My kids are the most important thing to me...I want to be there for every moment, to share in their joys and their struggles."

20- Kobe Bryant, former NBA player, was the father of four daughters before his tragic passing in 2020. He was a vocal advocate for fatherhood, stating "Being a father is the most rewarding thing in the world...it's a responsibility and a privilege, and I take it very seriously." Bryant also emphasized the importance of being present for his daughters, saying "I want to be there for every moment, to support them and guide them and be the best father I can be."

21- Russell Wilson, NFL player, is the father of two children. He has spoken about the importance of being a present and engaged father, saying "Being a father is the most important job in the world...I want to make sure that I'm there for my kids, to teach them and love them and help them become the best they can be."

22- Jay-Z, rapper and businessman, is the father of three children. He has spoken about how fatherhood has changed him, saying "I have a beautiful wife who's understanding and knows I'm not the worst of what I've done. The hardest thing is seeing pain on someone's face that you caused, and then have to deal with yourself. So, you know, most people don't want to do that. You don't want to look inside yourself."

23- J. Cole, rapper and producer, is the father of two children. He has spoken about his experience of becoming a father, saying "Being a father changes everything. It changes your perspective on everything. It's not about you anymore, it's about them. It's about what you can do to make their lives better. It's about being there for them, no matter what."

24- Carmelo Anthony, NBA player, is the father of one son. He has spoken about the importance of being present for his son's life, saying "My son is my motivation. I want to be there for him, to support him, to be his role model. It's not just about playing basketball, it's about being there for him as a father."

25- Tyrese Gibson, actor and musician, is the father of one daughter. He has spoken about the challenges he faced as a father, saying "Being a father is not easy. It's hard work, but it's the most rewarding work you'll ever do. You have to be there for your child, no matter what. You have to be their rock, their support system, their everything."

26- Ludacris, rapper and actor, is the father of three children. He has spoken about how fatherhood has changed him, saying "Fatherhood has made me a better person. It's made me more patient, more understanding, more loving. It's the greatest thing that's ever happened to me."

27- Anthony Anderson, actor and comedian, is the father of two children. He has spoken about the importance of being a father figure, saying "Being a father figure is not just about being there for your own kids, it's about being there for all kids. It's about setting an example, being a role model, and showing them that they can be anything they want to be."

28- Terry Crews, actor and former NFL player, is the father of five children. He has spoken about the importance of being present for his children, saying "I want my kids to know that they can always count on me. I want to be there for them, to support them, to love them, no matter what. That's what being a father is all about."

29- Tyler Perry, actor, director, and producer, is the father of one son. He has spoken about how his son has changed his life, saying "My son has given me purpose. He's given me a reason to get up in the morning, to work hard, to be the best father I can be. He's my everything."

30- Nas, rapper and entrepreneur, is the father of two children. He has spoken about how fatherhood has inspired his music, saying "Fatherhood has given me a new perspective on life. It's given me something to fight for, something to live for. It's inspired my music in ways I never thought possible."

31- Eddie Murphy, actor and comedian, is the father of ten children. He has spoken about how fatherhood has changed him, saying "Fatherhood has made me a better person. It's made me more patient, more understanding, more loving. It's the greatest thing that's ever happened to me."

32- Forest Whitaker, actor and producer, is the father of four children. He has spoken about how his children have inspired him to become a better person and father, saying "Being a father is a gift, it's an honor, it's a responsibility, it's a joy, it's a challenge. I'm blessed to have the opportunity to be a father and to have children who inspire me to be better every day."

33- Magic Johnson, retired NBA player and entrepreneur, is the father of three children. He has spoken about the importance of being present for his children, saying "You have to be there for your kids. You have to be a parent. That's what being a father is all about. It's not about the money or the fame. It's about being there for your kids and being a good role model."

34- Kenan Thompson, actor and comedian, is the father of two children. He has spoken about the joys of being a father, saying "Being a father is the best thing that has ever happened to me. It's a blessing to see your children grow and to be a part of their lives. I love being a dad and I wouldn't trade it for anything in the world."

35- Steve Harvey, comedian and talk show host, is the father of seven children. He has spoken about the importance of being a father figure to his children and to other young people, saying "Being a father is not just about having kids. It's about being a role model, a mentor, and a friend. It's about being there for your kids and for other young people who need guidance and support."

36- Samuel L. Jackson, actor and producer, is the father of one child. He has spoken about the importance of being present for his child, saying "Being a father is about being there for your child, no matter what. It's about showing up, being present, and being a positive influence in their life. It's the most important job you can have."

37- DJ Khaled, music producer and DJ, is the father of two children. He has spoken about the importance of being a positive role model for his children, saying "My son is my legacy. I want to make sure he understands that everything I do is for him and his future. I want him to know that anything is possible if you work hard and believe in yourself." Khaled frequently shares photos and videos of his children on social media, emphasizing the importance of family and fatherhood in his life.

38- Snoop Dogg, rapper and actor, is the father of four children. He has spoken about how his role as a father has changed his perspective on life, saying "Being a father has taught me to be more patient, more understanding, and more compassionate. It's not just about me anymore, it's about my children and their future." Snoop Dogg has been open about the challenges he has faced in balancing his career and family life, but continues to prioritize his children and their well-being.

39- Neil deGrasse Tyson, astrophysicist and author, is the father of two children. He has spoken about the importance of instilling a love of learning in his children, saying "I want my children to know that education is not just something you do in school, it's a lifelong pursuit. I want them to be curious, to ask questions, and to never stop learning." Tyson has also emphasized the importance of spending time with his children and being present in their lives, despite his busy schedule.

40- Timbaland, music producer and rapper, is the father of three children. He has spoken about the importance of setting a positive example for his children, saying 'I want my children to see that anything is possible if you believe in yourself and work hard. I want them to know that I support them in whatever they want to do, and that I'll always be there for them." Timbaland has been open about his struggles with addiction and mental health, and has emphasized the importance of seeking help and support when needed.

41- Jay Ellis, actor, is the father of one daughter. He has spoken about the joy of becoming a father and the importance of being present in his daughter's life, saying "Being a father has brought so much love and joy into my life. I want to be there for every moment, every milestone, and every memory. It's a privilege to be her dad." Ellis has also emphasized the importance of being a positive role model and setting a good example for his daughter.

42- Jesse Williams, actor and activist, is the father of two children. He has spoken about the importance of teaching his children about social justice and activism, saying "I want my children to know that they have a responsibility to make the world a better place. I want them to understand the power of their voice and their actions, and to never stop fighting for what is right." Williams has been vocal about his activism work, and has emphasized the importance of using his platform to create positive change in the world.

43- Sterling K. Brown, actor, is the father of two children. He has spoken about the importance of being present in his children's lives, saying "I don't want to miss a single moment. I want to be there for the good times and the bad, the happy moments and the sad. I want to be their dad, always and forever." Brown has been open about his own experiences with fatherhood and the impact it has had on his life and career.

44- Trevor Noah, comedian and talk show host, is the father of one son. He has spoken about the joy of becoming a father and the importance of setting a positive example for his son, saying "I want my son to see that anything is possible if you work hard and believe in yourself. I want to be a positive role model for him and teach him to be kind, compassionate, and empathetic towards others. Being a father has given me a new perspective on life and what really matters. It's not about fame or fortune, it's about being there for the people you love and making a positive impact on the world." Noah has also spoken about the challenges of balancing his busy career with his role as a father, but has emphasized the importance of prioritizing his family and making time for them.

45- Danny Glover, actor, is the father of one daughter and has spoken about the importance of being present for his child. He said "Being a father means everything to me. It's about being present, being there for your child, and being a role model for them. That's what I strive to do every day."

46- Jerry Rice, retired NFL player, is the father of three children and has spoken about the importance of leading by example as a father. He said "As a father, you have to lead by example. You have to show your children what it means to work hard, to be disciplined, and to be a good person. That's how you make a difference in their lives."

47- Jesse Jackson, civil rights activist, is the father of five children and has spoken about the importance of being a present father. He said "Being a father means being present, being involved, and being committed. It means being there for your children and showing them that you love them, no matter what."

48- Johnnie Cochran, attorney, was a dedicated father to his two children and often spoke about the importance of family. He said "Family is everything to me. Being a father means being there for your children, supporting them, and guiding them. It's the most important role you can have."

49- Kanye West, musician and entrepreneur, is the father of four children and has spoken about the transformative power of fatherhood. He said "Being a father changes everything. It changes your perspective, your priorities, and your purpose. It's the greatest blessing in the world."

50- Kareem Abdul-Jabbar, retired NBA player, is the father of five children and has spoken about the importance of being a positive influence on his children's lives. He said "Being a father means being a role model, being there for your children, and showing them that you care. It's about being a positive influence and helping them become the best versions of themselves."

51- Mike Tyson, the former heavyweight boxing champion, is the father of eight children. Despite his past controversies and battles with addiction, Tyson has been committed to being a present father for his children. In an interview, he said, "Being a father is the most rewarding thing you can ever do in your life. It's a constant challenge, but it's also the greatest thing you can do.

52- Louis Farrakhan, the leader of the Nation of Islam, is the father of nine children. He has spoken extensively about the importance of fatherhood in the black community, saying, "When a man becomes a father, he becomes a king in his own home. He is responsible for the destiny of his children."

53- Malcolm X, the civil rights leader and activist, was the father of six children. Despite his assassination at a young age,

Malcolm X's commitment to fatherhood was unwavering. He once said, "A man who stands for nothing will fall for anything. But a man who stands for his family and his children will never fall."

54- Martin Lawrence, the actor and comedian, is the father of three children. He has spoken about the importance of being present for his children, saying, "I make sure to take the time to be with my kids, to be there for them. They're the most important thing in my life."

55- Martin Luther King Jr., the civil rights icon, was the father of four children. He famously said, "The ultimate measure of a man is not where he stands in moments of comfort and convenience, but where he stands at times of challenge and controversy." King's commitment to his family and to the greater struggle for civil rights remains an inspiration to many.

56- Muhammad Ali, the legendary boxer, was the father of nine children. Despite his fame and success, Ali always made time for his children and spoke about the importance of fatherhood. He once said, "Children make you want to start life over."

57- Quincy Jones, legendary music producer and composer, is the father of seven children. He has spoken about the importance of being a present father and how it has impacted his own life, saying "Being a father is the greatest thing that ever happened to me. It changed everything. It gives you a different perspective on life. It's the most important job in the world."

58- Scottie Pippen, former NBA player, is the father of eight children. He has spoken about how being a father has changed him and the joy it brings him, saying "Being a father is the best thing that's ever happened to me. It's taught me a lot about patience, love, and responsibility. My children bring me so much joy and make me want to be the best version of myself."

59- Spike Lee, filmmaker and producer, is the father of two children. He has spoken about the importance of being present for his children and how it has influenced his work, saying "Being a father is everything to me. It's made me more compassionate, more understanding, and more aware of the world around me. My children inspire me to be a better filmmaker and a better person."

60- Sidney Poitier, actor and filmmaker, is the father of six daughters. He has spoken about the importance of instilling values in his children and being a positive role model, saying "As a father, it's important to teach your children values, to instill in them a sense of responsibility and compassion. It's about being a positive influence in their lives and showing them the way."

61- Stevie Wonder, musician and songwriter, is the father of nine children. He has spoken about the importance of being a present father and how it has impacted his music, saying "Being a father has given me a deeper appreciation for life and love. It's inspired some of my greatest music and has made me a better person overall."

62- Terrence Howard, actor and musician, is the father of five children. He has spoken about how being a father has helped him grow and mature, saying "Being a father is the most rewarding thing I've ever done. It's taught me so much about love and sacrifice, and has helped me grow into the man I am today."

63- Tiger Woods, professional golfer, is the father of two children. He has spoken about the importance of being a present father and how it has impacted his career, saying

"Being a father is the best thing that's ever happened to me. It's taught me how to be patient, how to prioritize, and how to be present in the moment. It's made me a better golfer and a better person."

64- Shaquille O'Neal, retired NBA player, has six children and has talked about the importance of being a father figure to them. He said "I've got six children, and they mean everything to me. They're my legacy. Being a father is the most important thing in my life."

65- John Doe, this is dedicated to all the average fathers that stories are not known. We want you to know that you are appreciated, and we honor your dedication to being a dad. May your light continue to shine bright, and may you always be there for your children, being the best dad you can be, forever.

As we close the final chapter of this book, it's clear that fatherhood is a path that is not for the faint-hearted. It's riddled with countless challenges and hurdles, especially for black fathers. But with unwavering perseverance and resolve, we can surpass these roadblocks and become the exemplary fathers that our children need. We must tirelessly push for the acknowledgement and backing of black fathers, striving to construct a society that honors all parents for their vital role in molding the next generation.

DISCLOSURE:

I would like to provide a disclosure for this book to ensure transparency and clarity for the reader. The views and opinions expressed in this manuscript are my own and do not necessarily reflect the views of any organization, institution, or publication. The information presented in this publication is based on my own research, knowledge, and experience, as well as reputable sources. However, I cannot guarantee the accuracy or completeness of the information provided.

It is important to note that the content of this book is intended for educational and informational purposes only and should not be construed as professional advice or guidance. Readers are encouraged to conduct their own research and seek the advice of qualified professionals before making any decisions based on the information presented here.

Furthermore, the information presented in this writing may not apply universally and may be influenced by various factors, including but not limited to cultural, social, and political differences. It is important to consider the context and limitations of the information presented when applying it to specific situations or contexts.

Finally, I would like to reiterate that the opinions expressed in this literary work are my own and do not necessarily represent the views of the publisher or any other individual or entity. Thank you for taking the time to read this disclosure and I hope that the information presented in this book is helpful and informative.

CONTACT INFORMATION

We'd love to hear from you! If you have any questions, comments, or feedback about the book or our merchandising, please don't hesitate to contact us. You can reach us by email at AtlasPressAd@gmail.com or Info@AtlasPressLLC.com. We appreciate your support and look forward to connecting with you!

I am so grateful for your support in reading my book. If you found value in its content and would like to support my continued writing endeavors, please consider making a small donation. My aim is to keep producing content that motivates and uplifts people while also providing for my family. Your donation will aid me in achieving these goals. You can reach us by email at

AtlasPressAd@gmail.com or Info@AtlasPressLLC.com.

Thank you for your generosity and belief in my work.

We eagerly await your success stories and insights about this book. Please feel free to send your letters and contributions to the following address.

Atlas Press Publishing, LLC

9206 Avenue K

Brooklyn, NY 11236

www.ingramcontent.com/pod-product-compliance
Lightning Source LLC
Chambersburg PA
CBHW071407120626
46546CB00002B/849